AA/Baedeker
Athens

D0562059

# Baedeker's

AA

# Athens

THE AUTOMOBILE ASSOCIATION

## Imprint

Cover picture: Acropolis

64 colour photographs
7 plans, 2 figures, 1 large city map

Text:
Dr Otto Gärtner

Conception and editorial work:
Redaktionsbüro Harenberg, Schwerte
English language: Alec Court

Cartography:
Ingenieurbüro für Kartographie Huber & Oberländer, Munich
Hallwag AG, Berne (city map)

General direction:
Dr Peter Baumgarten, Baedeker Stuttgart

English translation: James Hogarth

Source of illustrations:
dpa (9), Historia-Photo (12), Olympic (1), Rogge (27), Uthoff (15)

Following the tradition established by Karl Baedeker in 1844, sights of particular interest and hotels of particular quality are distinguished by either one or two asterisks.

To make it easier to locate the various sights listed in the "A to Z" section of the Guide, their coordinates on the large map of Athens are shown in red at the head of each entry.

Only a selection of hotels and restaurants can be given: no reflection is implied, therefore, on establishments not included.

In a time of rapid change it is difficult to ensure that all the information given is entirely accurate and up to date, and the possibility of error can never be entirely eliminated. Although the publishers can accept no responsibility for inaccuracies and omissions they are always grateful for corrections and suggestions for improvement.

© 1982 Baedeker Stuttgart
Original German edition

© 1982 Jarrold and Sons Ltd
English language edition worldwide

© The Automobile Association, 1982 60969
United Kingdom and Ireland

Licensed user:
Mairs Geographischer Verlag GmbH & Co., Ostfildern-Kemnat bei Stuttgart

Reproductions:
Gölz Repro-Service GmbH, Ludwigsburg

The name *Baedeker* is a registered trademark

Printed in Great Britain by Jarrold & Sons Ltd
Norwich

ISBN 0 86145 114 7

# Contents

## Preface

This Pocket Guide to Athens is one of the new generation of AA Baedeker guides.

These pocket-size city guides, illustrated throughout in colour, are designed to meet the needs of the modern traveller. They are quick and easy to consult, with the principal sights described in alphabetical order and practical details about opening times, how to get there, etc., shown in the margin.

Each guide is divided into three parts. The first part gives a general account of the city, its history, prominent personalities and so on; in the second part the principal sights are described; and the third part contains a variety of practical information designed to help visitors to find their way about and make the most of their stay.

The new guides are abundantly illustrated and contain numbers of newly drawn plans. In a pocket at the back of the book is a large city map, and each entry in the main part of the guide gives the coordinates of the square on the map in which the particular monument or site is situated. Users of this guide, therefore, will have no difficulty in finding what they want to see.

# Facts and Figures

## General

Capital

Athens is the capital of Greece (since 1834) and the seat of government, as well as the chief town of the district (Greek *nómos*) of Attica.

Greece

Greece – officially the Hellenic Republic – is the most southerly of the Balkan states, bounded oh the NW by Albania, on the N by Yugoslavia and Bulgaria and on the NE by Turkey. On the E it is washed by the Aegean, on the S by the Mediterranean and on the W by the Ionian Sea.
The Greek coastline has a total length of some 15,000 km (9300 miles). Greece has 185 inhabited islands, with a total area of 24,909 sq. km (9617 sq. miles), and numerous uninhabited islands (257 sq. km – 99 sq. miles).

Situation

Athens lies on the Saronic Gulf, on the S coast of the peninsula of Attica (central Greece), in longitude 23° 40′ E and latitude 37° 57′ N.

Area

Greater Athens has an area of 428 sq. km (165 sq. miles) and a population of 2·5 million (5935 per sq. km – 15,000 per sq. mile).
Greater Athens includes, in addition to the city itself, 21 outer communes, including Chalándri, Cháidari, Ekáli, Kallithéa, Kifissiá, Maroússi, Néo Fáliron, Paleó Fáliron and Piraeus. The oldest part of the city is the Pláka district.

Language

The language of Greece is modern Greek, written in the ancient Greek alphabet. There are two main variant forms, the more formal *katharévousa* and the colloquial *dimotikí* ("demotic"), now increasingly making its way as a literary language.

## Population and Religion

Population

Almost a quarter of the total population of Greece lives in the Athens area. Only a hundred years ago the town had no more than 124,000 inhabitants, compared with the 2·5 million people who now live in Greater Athens. It is estimated that some two out of every three Athenians come from the islands, from the villages on the Greek mainland or from Asia Minor.
The Greeks feel themselves to be the descendants of the Greeks of classical antiquity, but as a result of their many centuries of foreign rule their blood is mixed with that of many other peoples (Turks, Albanians, Bulgars, etc.).
Athens is home to many peoples, including Turks, Slavs, Vlachs, Albanians, Pomaks, Bulgarians, Armenians and gipsies.

◀ *The Acropolis: in the background Lykabettos*

Religion

In spite of the regional differences resulting from the vicissitudes of history and the country's extreme geographical fragmentation the Greeks have preserved a strong sense of their national identity. One great unifying force, particularly in times of hardship and oppression, has been the *Orthodox Church*, which is still a major influence in both the personal and the public life of the Greeks. The Greek church has been autonomous since 1833; since 1850 it has been recognised by the Oecumenical Patriarchate in Constantinople as autocephalous (appointing its own patriarchs); and since 1864 it has been the national ("established") Church of Greece.

The Greek Orthodox Church has 82 dioceses, the bishops of which are known as metropolitans. The Archbishop of Athens and All Greece is also head of the Greek Church and presides over the Holy Synod, a permanent body of 12 members, and over meetings of the "hierarchs" of the Church. Greek priests who wish to marry must do so before ordination. Those who marry will remain always at the level of parish priest. Those who wish to progress to the ranks of the higher clergy remain celibate.

The great majority of the population of Greece (97%) belong to the Greek Orthodox Church. There are also small groups – mainly foreigners – of Roman Catholics, Protestants, Jews and Moslems, as well as a variety of sects. All these religious minorities enjoy freedom of worship.

# Transport

Ports

There are two ports of Athens, at Piraeus and at Paleó Fáliro. Piraeus is now part of Greater Athens, and owing to its central situation has developed into the principal Greek port, the starting-point of almost all the boat services to the Greek islands and of numerous services to the western and eastern Mediterranean.

Airports

Athens has two airports at Ellinikón. The East Airport is used only by international airlines. The West or National Airport handles all services flown by the national airline, Olympic Airways.

Railways

The main station of Athens, the Larissa Station (Stathmós Larissis), is on the State Railways line from Piraeus via Athens to Salonica and Alexandroúpolis or on through Salonica into and through Europe. The Peloponnese Station is on the narrow-gauge Peloponnese Railway, which runs from Piraeus via Athens to Corinth and S through the Peloponnese to Kalamáta.

Bus services

Athens lies at the centre of the network of domestic bus services which link the city with towns and villages throughout the country.

There are also the bus services run by the State Railways. Within the city and suburbs of Athens there are yellow trolleybuses, and blue and green buses.

Electric Railway

This provides a fast service, running underground for part of the way, from Piraeus through central Athens to Kifissiá in the N and to Phaleron.

*People of Athens*

Athens is the starting-point of motorways (expressways) to Salonica and to Corinth and Patras.

Motorways

## Culture

Athens is the cultural centre of Greece, with its University and College of Technology, the Academy of Sciences, a Commercial College and Academy of Art, several libraries, including

General

11

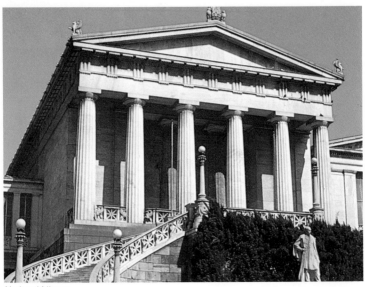

*National Library*

the National Library (photograph above) and the Gennadiós Library, a specialised library on Greece, and a whole range of museums of ancient and Byzantine culture, art galleries and natural history collections. Athens is also the headquarters of the Greek Archaeological Society and a number of foreign archaeological institutes, including the British School of Archaeology and the American School of Classical Studies.

Education

The educational reform of 1964 introduced free and compulsory schooling for six years from the age of six. The new consititution of 1975 provided for a nine-year period of compulsory schooling, due to be confirmed in 1981. In practice this has long been in operation.

Festivals

The Athens Festival is held annually in July–September in the Odeion of Herodes Atticus (see A to Z). The programme includes operatic and dramatic performances and concerts by leading Greek and international orchestras.

Theatres

Athens has some 40 theatres. A knowledge of modern Greek is, of course, necessary to appreciate the performances.
One of the few Karagiosis theatres still operating is the Hardimos theatre near the Monument of Lysikrátous (see A to Z). These shadow plays, derived from the Turkish Karagöz ("Black-Eye"), are played with coloured leather figures representing traditional stock types.

Cinemas

Many cinemas in Greece are open-air. Foreign films are usually shown in the original with Greek subtitles.

## Commerce and Industry

Greater Athens is the principal centre of industry and commerce (wholesale and specialist firms) in Greece, with the headquarters of most of the country's industrial enterprises and shipping companies and of all its banks. Of particular importance are the industrial installations on the Bay of Eleusis, the port and the insurance business. Athens is also an important centre of the tourist trade in Greece and the eastern Mediterranean.

General

The most important branches of industry are metalworking, textiles, foodstuffs and chemicals. The last industrial census showed that Athens had more than 42,000 industrial and craft firms with a total of over 279,000 workers; some 55,000 of the workers were in firms employing over 200, and there were some 2800 firms with more than 10 employees.

Industry

A principal element in the economy is the tourist trade. Visitors are attracted to Athens not only by the ancient sites in and around the city but also by the nearby bathing resorts on the Saronic Gulf.

# Prominent Figures in Greek History

Aeschylus was the founder of tragedy as we know it today: the history of European drama begins with him, for no plays written before his time have been preserved.

Aischylos/Aeschylus
(c. 525–c. 456 B.C.)

The tragedy was originally a "goat-song" (*tragos*, "goat", *odi*, "song") in honour of the god Dionysos. Earlier Thespis had put on performances with one actor and a chorus: Aeschylus' great innovation was to have two actors together with the chorus, thus making possible for the first time a dialogue and genuinely dramatic action. The chorus, limited to 12 members, was now reduced to the function of merely commenting on this dialogue. The main theme of the Aeschylean tragedies is the fateful tension between the gods and man, who is doomed to destruction if he rebels against the gods. Of Aeschylus' 90 tragedies five have been preserved complete: the "Persians", "Prometheus", the "Seven against Thebes", the "Suppliant Women" and the "Oresteia", a trilogy consisting of "Agamemnon", the "Libation-Bearers" and the "Eumenides".
Aeschylus was born in Eleusis and fought in the battle of Marathon (490 B.C.), as his epitaph recorded. After the success of the "Persians" (472 B.C.) he accepted an invitation from Hieron I, tyrant of Gela and Syracuse, to go to Sicily, but later returned to Athens. After coming into conflict with Pericles, who regarded the "Oresteia" as hostile criticism of himself, Aeschylus withdrew into voluntary exile at Gela.

13

## Prominent Figures in Greek History

**Alkibiades/Alcibiades**
(*c.* 450–*c.* 404 B.C.)

Alcibiades, a military leader and politician trained by the sophists, was a pupil and friend of Socrates and grew up in the house of his uncle Pericles. In 417–416 B.C. he led the Athenian attack on the neutral island of Melos, and in 415 he was the initiator of the fatal military expedition against Sicily. He then went to Sparta; in 408 he returned temporarily to Athens, and finally withdrew to Phrygia, where he was murdered at the behest of the Persian satrap.

**Antisthenes**
(*c.* 450–*c.* 360 B.C.)

Antisthenes was an enthusiastic follower of the philosopher Socrates. Soon after Socrates' death he founded the philosophical school of the Cynics (from *kynikos*, "dog-like", i.e. with no more needs than a dog). Antisthenes preached a philosophy of deliberate poverty and the reduction of human needs to a minimum. The Cynics were also known as "dog-like" because they fell upon men as dogs do and sought to convert them to their philosophy. From this the word "cynic" has degenerated to its present meaning.

**Aristophanes**
(*c.* 450–*c.* 386 B.C.)

Aristophanes was the leading writer of the Athenian "Old Comedy". Eleven of his 40 plays have been preserved, and some of them, including "Lysistrata", "The Birds", "Peace" and the "Acharnians", are still performed.

**Aristoteles/Aristotle**
(384–322 B.C.)

Aristotle, a native of Stageira (Macedonia), was a pupil of Plato at the Academy from 367 to 348 B.C. and thereafter went to Macedonia as tutor to Alexander the Great, returning in 336 to Athens, where he founded a school of philosophy in the Lykeion (Lyceum). His pupils were known as Peripatetics after the *peripatos* (covered walk) of the Lykeion.
Out of his numerous works a number of systematic treatises have been preserved, covering logic, the natural sciences, metaphysics, ethics, politics and poetics. "Aristotle sought to study the actual scientific content of phenomena in order to achieve an understanding of their essential substance. He was the creator and organiser of the scientific division of labour" (Buchwald).

**Michael Choniates**
(*c.* 1138–*c.* 1222)

Michael Choniates, a native of Chonai in Asia Minor, became Archbishop of Athens in 1182, but fled to the island of Kea in 1204 to escape the Frankish conquerors of the fourth Crusade. Among other writings he composed an elegy on the city of Athens.

**Demokritos/Democritus**
(*c.* 460–*c.* 380 B.C.)

Democritus, a native of Abdera in Thrace, lived in Athens as a philosopher and scientist, developing his Atomist theory, which anticipated Locke's distinction between primary and secondary qualities.

**Demosthenes**
(384–322 B.C.)

Demosthenes, the most famous of the Attic orators, inveighed against Philip II and the powerful kingdom of Macedon. After the deaths of Philip and his son Alexander Demosthenes was condemned to death by Antipater and fled to the island of Kalaureia, where he took poison in the sanctuary of Poseidon in order to escape arrest.

**Diokles/Diocles of Karystos**
(4th c. B.C.)

Diocles, born in Karystos on the island of Euboea, was a member of the Sicilian school of doctors who lived in Athens and became the leading Greek physician after Hippocrates. His

*Euripides*

*King George I*

*King Otto I*

works, of which only fragments have survived, were concerned with human anatomy, women's diseases, the identification of symptoms of disease and the use of herbs.

Epicureanism is a philosophy which recognises the happiness of the individual as the sole human value and seeks to avoid whatever causes more pain than pleasure. This philosophy, however, was not in any sense an advocacy of unrestrained enjoyment: its ideals were withdrawal from the world, repose of the soul and friendship.
Epicurus, a native of Samos, founded his school in a garden in Athens in 1306, and his teachings became known as the "philosophy of the garden".

Epikouros/Epicurus
(341–270 B.C.)

Euripides was the founder of the psychological drama, the tragedy of character. He believed, with the sophist Protagoras, that man was the "measure of all things"; and in his tragedies it is no longer the gods who sway the fates of men but man himself who lives his own life and destroys himself or wrestles with his own very personal problems.
Of his 92 dramas 18 have been preserved, including "Alcestis" (438), "Medea" (431), the "Children of Heracles" (c. 430), "Andromache" (c. 429), "Hecuba" (c. 425), "Electra" (c. 413), "Heracles" (after 423), the "Trojan Women" (415), "Helena" (412), "Iphigenia in Tauris" (c. 412), "Orestes" (408), "Iphigenia in Aulis" (after 407–406), the "Bacchae" (after 407–406) and a satyric play, "Cyclops".
The plays of Euripides have influenced the whole development of drama in Europe. Almost all his dramas have been re-worked or imitated by later dramatists, from Corneille and Racine to Goethe and Schiller, Franz Grillparzer and Jean-Paul Sartre.

Euripides
(c. 480–c. 406 B.C.)

George I, elected king of Greece in 1863, was a Danish prince. He acquired the Ionian Islands, which were given up by Britain, and Thessaly, and in the Balkan wars of 1912–13 gained Macedonia and Salonica. He was murdered in Salonica in 1913.

George I
(1845–1913)

Herodes Atticus, a native of Marathon, spent much of his life in Athens, where he was a teacher of rhetoric and held various

Herodes Atticus
(c. A.D. 101–177)

important public offices. He employed his immense wealth in munificent benefactions, endowing Athens with a temple of Tyche, the Odeion (still preserved) which bears his name, on the S side of the Acropolis, and the marble Stadion (restored in the 19th c.), near which he was buried.

Iktinos/Ictinus
(5th c. B.C.)

Ictinus (place of origin unknown) was the architect of the Parthenon in Athens (449–438 B.C.), the classical Telesterion at Eleusis and the temple of Apollo at Phigaleia. He established the Attic style of architecture, a combination of Doric and Ionic elements.

Menandros/Menander
(342–291 B.C.)

Meander was the leading representative of the New Comedy. A native of Athens, he received his philosophical education from the Peripatetics (see Aristotle). Of his plays, over 100 in number, only one has survived complete, the comedy "Dyskolos" ("The Misanthrope"), with which he won a first prize in the dramatic contest of 316 B.C..

Miltiades
(c. 550–c. 489 B.C.)

Miltiades, son of Cimon, was the commander of the victorious Athenians and Plataeans in the battle of Marathon. He died from a wound received during the siege of the island of Paros (489 B.C.).

Myron
(mid 5th c. B.C.)

Myron was a native of Eleutherai but was regarded as an Athenian since he did most of his work as a sculptor and bronze-founder there. He was renowned for the lifelike quality of his sculpture, of which the Discus-Thrower and the group of Athena and Marsyas are known to us in copies.

Otto I
(1815–67)

Otto I, son of king Ludwig I of Bavaria, was the first king of Greece (1833–62). He ruled at first with a Regency Council and later as an absolute monarch, but in 1843 was compelled to grant a constitution. He promoted the building of the modern city of Athens and the development of Greece into a European state. He was deposed in 1862 and returned to Germany, where he died. He and his queen, Amalia, are buried in Munich.

Peisistratos/Pisistratus
(c. 600–528/527 B.C.)

Pisistratus, a native of Brauron, became tyrant of Athens in 560 B.C. and remained in power, apart from two periods of banishment, until his death. He introduced the cult of Dionysos, with regular performances of tragedies, maintained the laws of Solon, embellished Athens with temples and other buildings (temple of Athena, Olympieion), caused the Homeric epics to be collected and established the Panathenaic festival (see A to Z, Agora). He was succeeded by his sons Hippias and Hipparchus, under whom the ancient Greek "tyranny" (a usurped monarchy) became a tyranny in the modern sense.

Perikles/Pericles
(c. 495–429 B.C.)

Pericles, Athens' greatest statesman, gave his name to the city's glorious heyday, the "age of Pericles".
In 472 B.C. he was *choregos* ("leader" of the choris, who met its expenses) in a performance of Aeschylus' "Persians". In 461 he became leader of the democratic party, and in 443 the sole ruler and elected military leader of Athens.
In 454 he transferred the treasury of the Attic League from the island of Delos to Athens and used it to finance the construction of the new buildings on the Acropolis, which was now given its classical form.

With his mistress Aspasia, he promoted the arts and sciences, and was a friend of the sculptor Phidias, the philosopher Anaxagoras and the dramatist Sophocles. In 431 he was responsible for the outbreak of the Peloponnesian War. He died of plague in 429.

Phidias was already recognised in ancient times as the greatest sculptor of the classical period of Athens. He was entrusted by Pericles with the general direction of the great building programme on the Acropolis, for which he created the bronze statue of Athena Promachos and the chryselephantine (gold and ivory) statue of Athena Parthenos in the Parthenon. He was also responsible for some of the architectural sculpture on the Parthenon. No less renowned than the Athena Parthenos was his chryselephantine seated figure of Zeus at Olympia. In 432–431 B.C. he was accused of misappropriating gold intended for the statue of Athena, and is believed to have died in prison.

Pheidias/Phidias
(5th c. B.C.)

Plato, the greatest philosopher of ancient Greece, was a native of Athens and a scion of the Attic nobility. He was a pupil of Socrates for eight years, until his master's death in 399 B.C. After travelling in Sicily he returned to Athens and in 387 founded his school, the Academy, in form a cultic association but in practice a place of philosophical study and education. The central feature of Plato's philosophy is the theory of ideas. His works, 36 in number, are preserved complete. With the exception of the "Apology of Socrates" they are all in dialogue form.

Platon/Plato
(c. 427–c. 347 B.C.)

Praxiteles, who ranked with Scopas and Lysippus as one of the leading sculptors of his day, came of a family of Athenian sculptors and was a pupil of his father Cephisodotus. He worked mainly in marble but also produced work in bronze. Particularly famous in antiquity were his Aphrodite of Cnidos, Hermes with the boy Dionysos at Olympia, Apollo Sauroctonus (the lizard-slayer) and a wounded Amazon – masterpieces of the post-classical style.

Praxiteles
(4th c. B.C.)

Heinrich Schliemann was born in Mecklenburg and began his working life in a commercial business in Amsterdam. In 1847 he established his own business in St Petersburg and made a large fortune. After extensive travels he took up the study of archaeology in Paris in 1866. He discovered Troy, Mycenae and other Mycenaean sites, and in 1879 took up residence with his Greek wife Sophia in Athens, in a palatial mansion built for him by Ernst Ziller. He died in Naples and was buried in the principal cemetery of Athens.

Heinrich Schliemann
(1822–90)

Socrates, an Athenian of the deme of Alopece, was married late in life to Xanthippe, who acquired a legendary reputation as a shrew. In 406 B.C., as a *prytanis* (member of a committee of the Council) he defended the rule of law against the will of the popular assembly, and achieved prominence as a philosopher questing for truth in discussion in the Agora and in groups of friends. He never wrote down his teachings, which we know only from the works of his pupils, in particular Plato. In 399 he was condemned to death by drinking hemlock for the corruption of youth. He refused to seek safety in flight and died in the state prison in the Agora, surrounded by his pupils.

Sokrates/Socrates
(c. 470–c. 399 B.C.)

## Prominent Figures in Greek History

**Solon**
(*c.* 640–*c.* 560 B.C.)

The Athenian statesman and poet Solon was later ranked among the Seven Sages of antiquity. As archon (the highest official of Athens) in 594 B.C. he forbade borrowing on the security of the borrower's person and abolished serfdom. He gave Athens a constitution, laid down the rights of the Areopagos and reformed the currency and the weights and measures of Athens. Then, after making the Athenians swear not to alter his constitution during his absence, he travelled extensively in Egypt and elsewhere.

**Sophokles/Sophocles**
(*c.* 496–*c.* 406 B.C.)

Sophocles was the second of the great Attic tragic dramatists, coming after Aeschylus and before Euripides. He introduced a third actor (see Aeschylus) and reduced the representation of the chorus still further, thus making possible the representation of real characters. It was left to Euripides, however, to achieve the psychological representation of character, for in Sophocles man is not yet the "measure of all things" but is still subject to the authority of all-powerful gods. Caught in the bonds of fate, man must struggle and suffer until at last, after this process of "learning through suffering", the smallness and impotence of man in face of the gods is made manifest.

Three of the seven dramas by Sophocles which have survived are concerned with the myth of Oedipus – "Oedipus the King", "Oedipus at Colonus" and "Antigone". His other plays are "Ajax", the "Trachinian Women", "Electra" and "Philoctetes".

**Themistokles/Themistocles**
(*c.* 528–*c.* 462 B.C.)

The Attic statesman Themistocles, archon in 493, initiated the development of Piraeus into a fortified port, and in 483 persuaded the Athenians to use the profits of the Laurion silver mines for the construction of warships, thus making possible the defeat of the Persian fleet at Salamis in 480. In 479 he fortified Athens. In 474, however, he was "ostracised" and expelled from Athens, and later died at Magnesia (Asia Minor), which was presented to him by the Persians.

**Thoukydides/Thucydides**
(*c.* 455–*c.* 400 B.C.)

Thucydides, founder of the science of history, came of a noble family. His "History of the Peloponnesian War", begun immediately after the outbreak of war (431 B.C.), describes and interprets the course of the conflict down to 411–410 B.C. Characteristic features of his work are his concern to achieve objectivity (in spite of his leaning towards the Athenian side), and an understanding of the events of the war through study of the circumstances of the events themselves.

**Xenokrates/Xenocrates**
(4th c. B.C.)

Xenocrates, a native of Chalcedon, studied at Plato's Academy from 378 B.C. onwards and became head of the Academy, in succession to Plato himself. He sought to reduce Plato's writings to a system.

**Xenophon**
(*c.* 430–*c.* 355 B.C.)

Xenophon, an Athenian, was a pupil of Socrates. After Socrates' death he was banished from Athens for supporting the Persians. He probably died in Corinth.

Among his works are the "Anabasis" (an account of the expedition of 10,000 Greek mercenaries through Asia Minor to Mesopotamia and back to the Black Sea) and the "Hellenica" (a history of Greece from 411 to 362, continuing Thucydides).

# History of Athens

## Mythology

Athens, aware of its high antiquity, honoured a series of mythical kings as its earliest rulers. According to the tradition recorded by Apollodorus and others the first king of Athens was Kekrops, who had the body of a snake and was credited with the first census of the population, the first laws, the introduction of monogamy and the invention of the alphabet. In his reign took place the contest between Poseidon and Athena for the land of Attica, a contest from which Athena emerged victorious. The tomb of Kekrops was incorporated into the Erechtheion (see A to Z, Acropolis) and is now under the Caryatid Porch. Close by is an olive-tree, marking the spot where Athena is said to have planted the first olive-tree.

Kekrops was succeeded by Pandion, who reigned in the period of Greek's great Flood. The sixth king was Pandion's son Erechtheus, whose stronghold is mentioned by Homer (II, 7, 81). His twin brother Boutes was a priest of Athena and Poseidon, whose cult was later celebrated in the Erechtheion. Erechtheus was succeeded by his descendants Kekrops II and Pandion II, the latter of whom was driven out and fled to Megara. His son Aegeus returned to Athens. The Aegean Sea is named after Aegeus, who threw himself into the sea when he saw the Athenian fleet returning with black sails and believed that his son Theseus' expedition had been unsuccessful.

This Theseus, the great hero of Athens, was the tenth of the mythical kings. The bringing together of the whole population of Attica in the city state of Athens (the "synoecism") is attributed to him. Travelling from Troizen, his birthplace, along the Saronic Gulf to Athens, he destroyed a series of robbers and monsters like Procrustes; and by killing the Minotaur he ended the payment of tribute by Athens to the Cretan king Minos. With his friend Peirithoos he fought the centaurs, with Herakles he fought the Amazons. He carried off the young Helen from Sparta to Aphidna in Attica. Finally he was killed on the island of Skyros by his host, king Lykomedes. About 475 B.C. Kimon brought his remains to Athens and built the Theseion in his honour.

The last king of Theseus' line was Thymoites, who passed on the crown to Melanthos, who had been driven out of Pylos by the invading Dorians, in gratitude for his military help. Melanthos was succeeded by his son Kodros, whose sacrificial death in 1068 B.C. saved Athens from the Dorian attack.

According to one tradition Kodros was the last of the kings. According to others he was succeeded by his son Medon, while other sons initiated the Greek settlement of the W coast of Asia Minor, Neleus being honoured as the founder of Miletus, Androklos as the founder of Ephesus.

These mythical traditions reflect the history of Athens from the early Mycenaean period to the beginning of the 1st millennium B.C. The history of the site, however, reaches much further back in time.

## Chronology

| | |
|---|---|
| *c.* 3000 B.C. | First traces of settlement on the southern slopes of the Acropolis and in the Agora area. These pre-Greeks were traditionally known as "Pelasgians". |
| *c.* 2000 B.C. | Indo-European peoples move into the Aegean mainland area and subjugate the Pre-Greeks. |
| *c.* 1400 B.C. | The Acropolis becomes a fortified royal citadel covering an area of 35,000 sq. m – 42,000 sq. yd (Mycenae 30,000 sq. m – 36,000 sq. yd, Tiryns 20,000 sq. m – 24,000 sq. yd). |
| 1200 B.C. | The Dorians bypass Attica. Athens takes in refugees from the Peloponnese. Population pressure leads to the establishment of colonies in western Asia Minor and on the islands off its coasts. |
| 9th c. B.C. | The noble families of Attica take up residence in Athens. |
| 8th c. B.C. | Emergence of an oligarchic state. The functions of the king are taken over by archons, appointed for a year at a time from members of the great families. The Areopagos is established, its membership consisting of former archons. |
| 620 B.C. | Drakon (Draco) is the first to codify the laws of Attica. The severe penalties provided for in his laws have given us the word "draconic". |
| 594–593 B.C. | Solon abolishes servitude for debt and gives Athens a new constitution. The population is divided into four groups according to fiscal status. The Council of 400 is established alongside the Areopagos. |
| 560 B.C. | Peisistratos, a native of Brauron, becomes "tyrant" (sole ruler) of Athens, which enjoys a period of prosperity under his rule. |
| 528–527 B.C. | Peisistratos dies and is succeeded by his sons Hippias and Hipparchos. |
| 514 B.C. | Hippias is murdered. |
| 510 B.C. | Fall of the tyranny: Hipparchos is expelled from Athens. |
| 508–507 B.C. | Kleisthenes reforms the state; establishment of democracy. The population of Attica is divided into ten tribes (*phylai*), which appoint 50 members each to the Council of 500. Introduction of ostracism. |
| 490 B.C. | The Athenians defeat the Persians at Marathon. Themistokles secures approval of his fleet-building programme. |
| 480 B.C. | The Persians, under Xerxes, again invade Greece, break through at Thermopylai and devastate Athens and the Acropolis. Athens defeats the Persian fleet at Salamis. |
| 479 B.C. | Final victory over the Persians (battles of Plataiai and Mykale). Building of the Themistoclean Walls. |

| | |
|---|---|
| Perikles becomes the dominant figure in Athens: beginning of the "age of Perikles". Building programme on the Acropolis. | 461 B.C. |
| Perikles concludes a 30 years' armistice with Sparta. | 445 B.C. |
| Peloponnesian War between Athens and Sparta. The war ends in the defeat of Athens (destruction of the Attic fleet at Aigospotamoi). Sparta establishes the rule of the "Thirty Tyrants" in Athens. | 431–404 B.C. |
| Death of Perikles. | 429 B.C. |
| Sokrates is condemned to death. | 399 B.C. |
| Establishment of the second Attic Maritime League. | 377 B.C. |
| Philip II of Macedon establishes his authority over the whole of Greece at the battle of Chaironeia. | 338 B.C. |
| Philip of Macedon is murdered. | 336 B.C. |
| Alexander the Great consolidates Macedonian authority in Greece and establishes a world empire. | 336–323 B.C. |
| Death of Alexander the Great. | 323 B.C. |
| Large building enterprises by Hellenistic kings of Pergamon and Syria: Stoa of Attalos, Stoa of Eumenes, work on Olympieion. | 2nd c. B.C. |
| Greece becomes a Roman province. | 146 B.C. |
| The Apostle Paul preaches in Athens. | A.D. 50 |
| The Emperor Hadrian founds the "city of Hadrian" around the Olympieion, which he completes. | 117–138 |
| The Herulians, an eastern Germanic people, devastate Athens. The "Valerian Wall" is built to protect the much reduced area of the city. | 267 |
| A large Gymnasion is built in the Agora to house the University of Athens. | Around 400 |
| The Christian Emperor of the East, Theodosius II, orders the closing of pagan places of worship. Some of the temples (the Temple of Hephaistos) are converted into churches. The first purpose-built churches are erected. | 426 |
| The Emperor Justinian closes Athens University and Plato's Academy. | 529 |
| Athens becomes the see of an archbishop. | 869 |
| The Emperor Basil II visits Athens, now no more than a small country town – the only Byzantine emperor to do so. | 1085 |
| After the fourth Crusade Athens becomes the residence of a Frankish duke, who converts the Propylaia on the Acropolis into his palace. | 1203–4 |

## History of Athens

| | |
|---|---|
| 1311 | Catalan mercenaries occupy the town. |
| 1446 | The Venetians occupy Athens. |
| 1456 | Sultan Mehmet II conquers Athens. The Parthenon becomes a mosque. Beginning of the Turkish period. |
| 1668 | French Capuchin friars incorporate the Monument of Lysikrates in their convent. |
| 1674 | De Nointel, French ambassador in Constantinople, visits Athens and has drawings made of the ancient remains. |
| 1687 | A Venetian, Morosini, takes the Acropolis. A Venetian grenade destroys the Parthenon. |
| 1821 | The Greek war of independence begins. Athens is taken by rebel Greek forces. |
| 1826 | The Turks retake Athens. |
| 1830 | The three great powers – Britain, France and Russia – declare Greece to be an independent sovereign kingdom. |
| 1832 | The powers recognise the Bavarian prince Otto of Wittelsbach as king of Greece. |
| 1833 | The Turks finally leave Athens (12 April). Otto of Bavaria, first king of Greece, arrives. |
| 1834 | King Otto I makes Athens capital of Greece. |
| 1843 | After a bloodless military rising Greece becomes a constitutional monarchy. |
| 1862 | King Otto I is deposed. |
| 1864 | The Danish prince William George of Glücksburg is elected king as George I. |
| 1911–13 | Balkan Wars. Greece wins Epirus, Macedonia, Crete and Samos. |
| 1913 | George I is murdered in Salonica. Succeeded by Constantine. |
| 1923 | After the Greek defeat in the war with Turkey, Athens has to take in some 300,000 refugees from Asia Minor. Whole new districts are developed. |
| 1924 | George II is deposed. Greece becomes a republic. |
| 1935 | Restoration of the monarchy. George II returns to the throne. |
| 1941 | Germany invades Greece. A government in exile is set up in London. |
| 1944 | Liberation of Athens. Beginning of civil war. |
| 1949 | The civil war ends in the defeat of the Communists. |

| | |
|---|---|
| Military putsch: the military government of Papadopoulos comes to power. After an unsuccessful attempt at a counter-putsch King Constantine II leaves Greece. | 1967 |
| President Gizikis brings Constantine Karamanlis back from exile as Prime Minister. | 1974 |
| New republican constitution. | 1975 |
| Greece becomes a member of the European Community. | 1981 |

# Quotations

"Now while Paul waited for them at Athens, his spirit was stirred in him, when he saw the city wholly given to idolatry. Therefore disputed he in the synagogue with the Jews, and with the devout persons, and in the market daily with them that met with him. Then certain philosophers of the Epicureans, and of the Stoicks, encountered him. And some said, What will this babbler say? other some, He seemeth to be a setter forth of strange gods: because he preached unto them Jesus, and the resurrection. And they took him, and brought him unto Areopagus, saying, May we know what this new doctrine, whereof thou speakest, is? For thou bringest certain strange things to our ears: we would know therefore what these things mean. (For all the Athenians and strangers which were there spent their time in nothing else, but either to tell, or to hear some new thing.)

"Then Paul stood in the middle of Mars' hill, and said, Ye men of Athens, I perceive that in all things ye are too superstitious. For as I passed by, and beheld your devotions, I found an altar with this inscription, TO THE UNKNOWN GOD. Whom therefore ye ignorantly worship, him declare I unto you. . . .

"Howbeit certain men clave unto him, and believed: among the which was Dionysius the Areopagite, and a woman named Damaris, and others with them."

*Acts of the Apostles (c. A.D. 63) 17, 16–23 and 34*

"The inhabitants of this country have on every occasion given splendid and most admirable examples of their disposition, now displaying in the mildness of their manners and in their social intercourse what can truly be called humanity (and no others can aspire to equal them in goodness), now in times of danger and difficulty facing up to the enemy as champions of Greece. And indeed, when we consider the land and the sea, the form of Attica is calculated to bring this about. For it lies in front of Greece like a bulwark, extending eastward in a peninsula to assert the advanced position which has been assigned to it. It is easy to believe that it was created by the gods for the protection of Hellas, and that it alone was destined by nature to stand at the head of the Greek world."

*Aelius Aristides Greek sophist (c. 117–c. 187) "Panathenaikos", 95–7*

"From the summit of the Acropolis I watched the sun rise between the two peaks of Mount Hymettus. The crows which nest round the citadel but never fly over it floated in the air below us, their brilliant black wings tinged with pink by the first light of dawn. Columns of light bluish vapour rose from the

*François-René de Chauteaubriand French writer (1768–1848) "Itinéraire de Paris à Jérusalem"*

*Chateaubriand*

*Cicero*

*Herodotus*

shadows on the flanks of Hymettus, signalling the presence of gardens and beehives. Athens, the Acropolis and the ruins of the Parthenon were bathed in a delicate peach-blossom hue. The sculptures of Phidias, caught in a horizontal beam of golden light, came to life and seemed to be moving, thanks to the changing play of light and shadow on the contours of the marble.''

Marcus Tullius Cicero
Roman writer
(106–43 B.C.)

Herakleides
Greek philosopher
(*c.* 388–*c.* 310 B.C.)
Fragments

''There is no end to it in this city: wherever you set your foot, you encounter some memory of the past.''

''The city is very dry and has a poor water supply. The streets are irregular, since the city is so old. At first sight strangers may doubt whether this is indeed the famous city of the Athenians; but they will soon come to believe that it is. For here they will see the fairest things in the world. The theatre is large, imposing and beautiful. The temple of Athena is magnificent, raised high above the world and of great beauty: one is seized with amazement at sight of it. It stands above the theatre and is known as the Parthenon. The Olympieion is only half finished, but the plan of the building makes a profound impression: were it completed it would be a most splendid structure. There are three gymnasia: the Academy, the Lykeion and the Gymnasion of Kynosarges, all set amid trees and lawns. Here too there are all kinds of festivals, entertainment and edification from the philosophers, a variety of pastimes and regular dramatic performances.''

Herodotus
Greek historian
(*c.* 490–*c.* 425 B.C.)

''On this Acropolis there is a temple of Erechtheus, the Earth-Born, as he is called, and within its precinct are an olive-tree and a pool containing sea-water. The Athenians say that these were put there by Athena and Poseidon during their contest for the land of Attica in token of their taking possession of the land. The olive-tree, however, met the same fate as the rest of the sanctuary: it was burned down by the barbarians. But when on the day after the fire some Athenians went up to the sanctuary to perform a sacrifice at the behest of the Persian king they saw a shoot which had sprung from the stump of a tree to the height of a cubit. And of this they spread the report in the city.''

"So far has our city surpassed the rest of mankind in the field of thinking and speaking that her pupils have become the teachers of other men. So much is this so that the name of Hellenes no longer appears to betoken a particular race, but rather a disposition of mind, and is applied to those who share our culture rather than those who share our descent."

Isokrates
Greek orator
(436–338 B.C.)
"Panegyrikos"

(In a letter to Eduard von Schenck)
"Few houses in the town, and few of the trees in the many gardens once to be found here, have been spared: the Turks are masters in the art of destruction. But the town is rising again with remarkable speed; and though there may be reason to be satisfied with the quantity of the houses the same cannot be said of their quality. Athens has now a very strange aspect: Europeans from every country in the continent, Germans of almost every race and Bavarians of all sorts and conditions rub shoulders with Americans, Turks, Moors and the Greeks themselves; and to all this are added the camels and the palms (of which some few have survived). In Hermes Street, which is the main street – though without a suspicion of paving, rough and rutted, worse than a country lane – you find an inn with a signboard in Greek, German and French, shops belonging to Frank and Bernau of Munich – and now you find me, lodging with my son. This may make you feel at home; but yet it is a strange world of its own, with the ruins left by both Greeks and Romans."

King Ludwig I of Bavaria
(1786–1868)

"Athens, the eye of Greece, mother of arts
And eloquence, native to famous wits
Or hospitable, in her sweet recess,
City of suburban, studious walks and shades;
See there the olive grove of Academe,
Plato's retirement, where the Attic bird
Trills her thick-warbled notes the summer long."

John Milton
English poet
(1608–74)

"That which was the chief delight of the Athenians and the wonder of strangers, and which alone serves for a proof that the boasted power and opulence of ancient Greece is not an idle tale, was the magnificence of the temples and public edifices. Yet no part of the conduct of Pericles moved the spleen of his enemies more than this. . . .
"Pericles answered . . . that as the state was provided with all the necessaries of war, its superfluous wealth should be laid out on such works as, when executed, would be eternal monuments of its glory, and which, during their execution, would diffuse a universal plenty; for as so many kinds of labour, and such a variety of instruments and materials were requisite to these undertakings, every art would be exerted, every hand employed, almost the whole city would be in pay, and be at the same time both adorned and supported by itself. . . .
"Thus works were raised of an astonishing magnitude, and inimitable beauty and perfection, every architect striving to surpass magnificence of the design with the elegance of the execution; yet still the most wonderful circumstance was the expedition with which they were completed. Many edifices, each of which seems to have required the labour of several successive ages, were finished during the administration of one prosperous man. . . .
"Hence we have the more reason to wonder, that the structures

Plutarch
Greek philosopher and
historian

*Prince von Pückler-Muskau*  *Ludwig I of Bavaria*

raised by Pericles should be built in so short a time, and yet built for ages: for as each of them, as soon as finished, had the venerable air of antiquity, so, now they are old, they have the freshness of a modern building."
(Langhorne translation)

Prince Hermann von
Pückler-Muskau
German writer
(1785–1871)

"A curse condemning them to be ridiculous seems to have been pronounced on the buildings of modern Athens, both public and private. Thus the Ministry of War and Marine has all the appearance of a warehouse, while the royal stables (let us hope a purely temporary structure) reminded me of the establishment of a Berlin bricklayer who has made his pile. . . .
"But in excavating foundations for these houses of cards the workmen smash to pieces the most magnificent old marble pavements and the other ancient remains of which the soil of Athens is so full. It is a real misfortune that the new city is being built on the same site as the ancient one; for this will bury for ever immense treasures of which we know nothing. It is true that the government has ordered that a small open space should be left round each of the monuments that are still standing; but apart from the fact that the government's orders are not universally respected, this does not go nearly far enough.
"It may be hoped, however, that at least the king's new palace, lying outside the town at the foot of Lycabettus (where once stood the school of the Cynics), will prove an honourable exception."

Synesios of Kyrene
Greek philosopher
(c. A.D. 370–c. 412)
Epistula 135

"Accursed be the shipmaster who brought me here! For present-day Athens has nothing left to claim our admiration except its famous name. And just as after a sacrificial animal has been consumed, nothing remains to remind us of it but its skin, so now in this Athens from which philosophy has fled we can but go about the town and admire, perhaps, the Academy and the Lykeion and the Painted Stoa which gave its name to the philosophy of Chrysippos, though the stoa has lost its paintings. . . . Nowadays it is Egypt that takes up and nurtures the philosophical seed of Hypatia, while Athens, once the haunt of the wise, now appeals only to beekeepers."

"Our constitution does not copy the laws of neighbouring states; we are rather a pattern to others than imitators ourselves. Its administration favours the many instead of the few; this is why it is called a democracy. . . .

"We provide plenty of means for the mind to refresh itself from business. We celebrate games and sacrifices all the year round, and the elegance of our private establishments forms a daily source of pleasure and helps to banish the spleen. . . .

"At Athens we live exactly as we please, and yet are just as ready to encounter every legitimate danger . . . and we have the double advantage of escaping the experience of hardships in anticipation and of facing them in the hour of need as fearlessly as those who are never free from them.

"Nor are these the only points in which our city is worthy of admiration. We cultivate refinement without extravagance and knowledge without effeminacy; wealth we employ more for use than for show, and place the real disgrace of poverty not in owning to the fact but in declining the struggle against it. . . .

"In short, I say that as a city we are the school of Hellas; while I doubt if the world can produce a man, who where he had only himself to depend upon, is equal to so many emergencies, and graced by so happy a versatility as the Athenian."
(Crawley translation)

Thucydides
Greek historian
(*c.* 455–*c.* 400 B.C.)
From the Funeral Oration of Perikles

"There is excellent foundation for the belief that the city lies approximately in the centre of Greece. For the farther one goes from Athens the more trying does the cold or the heat become; and a man travelling from one end of Greece to the other must pass by way of Athens, as the point at the centre of a circle."

Xenophon
Greek writer
(*c.* 430–*c.* 355 B.C.)
"Ways and Means", 6

# Athens from A to Z

## Academy of Plato (Akademía Plátonos) and Kolonós Hippios   A1

**Situation**
Kimonos Street
(W of railway station)

**Bus**
62

The Academy – probably named after the hero Hekademos, who had a cult grove here – lay 1·5 km ( 1 mile) NW of the Dipylon (a double fortified gateway with two inner and two outer towers, see Kerameikos), with which it was linked by a road 40 m (130 ft) wide. From 387 B.C. onwards this was the meeting-place of Plato and his pupils, the first academy in the world.

Excavations in this outlying district of Athens, beyond the railway line, have revealed remains of a square hall (between Efklídou and Tripóleos Streets), immediately N of this a small temple which may have been dedicated to the hero Hekademos, and a large complex of the Roman imperial period built round an inner courtyard. Here, too, was found a structure measuring 8.50 by 4.50 m (28 by 15 ft) now roofed over, the oldest building so far discovered in Athens, dating from the Early Bronze Age (2300–2100 B.C.).

From the area of the Academy Tripóleos Street runs NW to the nearby hill of Kolonós Hippios, which gave its name to the deme (district) of Kolonos, home of the great dramatist Sophocles (496–406 B.C.) and the setting of his play "Oedipus on Kolonos", written at the age of 90. The hill is now surrounded by a rather poor quarter of Athens. On it are tombstones commemorating two 19th c. archaeologists, Carl Otfried Müller (1797–1840 and François Lenormant (1837–83).

## Achárnes

**Bus**
60

**Distance**
12 km (7½ miles) N

The site of Achárnes was occupied from Mycenaean times, and in the classical period, as Acharnai, it was a place of some consequence. It is the setting of Aristophanes' comedy "The Acharnians".

The village (pop. 3000) is reached from Omónia Square by way of Vathis Square and Liossion Street.

3 km (2 miles) S of Achárnes, on the W side of the road, is a Mycenaean tholos tomb.

The ancient acropolis was on a hill to the W.

## * *Acropolis   C2/3

**Electric Railway**
Theseion station

**Bus**
16

A great crag of limestone rising out of the plain of Attica offered a site well adapted for the Acropolis, the fortified citadel of Athens. At first it served both as the stronghold of the kings of Athens and as the site of the city's oldest shrines; later it was reserved for the service of the divinities of Athens alone. This religious centre of ancient Athens, which received its classical

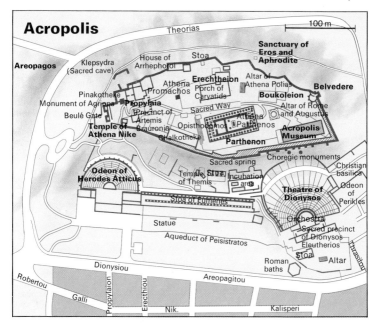

Acropolis

100 m

Theorias

Areopagos

Klepsydra
(Sacred cave)

House of
Arrhephoroi

Stoa

Sanctuary of
Eros and
Aphrodite

Erechtheion

Athena
Promachos

Porch of
Caryatids

Altar of
Athena Polias

Belvedere

Pinakotheke

Propylaia

Boukoleion

Monument of Agrippa

Precinct of

Sacred Way

Altar of Rome
and Augustus

Beulé Gate

Artemis
Brauronia

Opisthodomos

Athena
Parthenos

Acropolis
Museum

Temple of
Athena Nike

Halkotheke

Parthenon

Choregic monuments

Christian
basilica

Odeon of
Herodes Atticus

Sacred spring

Temple
of Themis

Stoa

Incubation
area

Theatre of
Dionysos

Odeon
of
Perikles

Stoa of Eumenes

Orchestra

Statue

Sacred precinct
of Dionysos
Eleutherios

Aqueduct of Peisistratos

Stoa

Altar

Roman
baths

Dionysiou

Areopagitou

Robertou

Galli

Propylaion

Erechthiou

Nik.

Kalisperi

form in the time of Pericles, thus reflected the humane values of Greek culture and thought which have retained their power down to our own day. In spite of the destruction wrought by many centuries, most notably the devastating explosion in 1687, when a Venetian grenade blew up a Turkish powder magazine which had been housed in the Parthenon and made the 2000-year-old temple a ruin, the surviving remains still convey something of the splendour of the age of Pericles.

During the 19th and early 20th c. the removal of post-classical structures and extensive works of restoration revealed the remains of the classical buildings of the 5th c. B.C. This process began in 1836, immediately after the liberation from Turkish rule, with the restoration (by Ludwig Ross, a German archaeologist on King Otto's staff) of the temple of Athena Nike, which had been incorporated in a Turkish bastion, and culminated in the re-erection of the columns on the N side of the Parthenon in the 1920s.

But the 20th c. has also contrived to wreak more destruction than the Acropolis had suffered in the preceding two and a half millennia. The fumes and pollution created by the swarming population and constant traffic of a great modern city, the damage caused by the landing and taking off of aircraft (which are now forbidden to overfly the Acropolis), and the three million visitors who climb up to the Acropolis every year have worn down the surface of the rock and the marble facing of the monuments, while the marble itself has suffered chemical change and the surviving classical sculpture (e.g. on the W

**Opening times**
Mon.–Sat. 8 a.m.–8 p.m.
Sun. 10 a.m.–4.30 p.m.

29

frieze of the Parthenon) is flaking away – all this at an alarming pace and on a disturbing scale.

Accordingly UNESCO set up a 15-million-dollar programme to save the Acropolis. The first steps have been to lay a wooden gangway through the Propylaia and to exclude the public from the structures flanking the Propylaia and the interior of the Parthenon. The caryatids have been removed from the Erechtheion – swathed during this process in scaffolding – and placed in the Acropolis Museum, where they can be protected from further damage.

How far the measures already taken and the others which are planned will contribute to the preservation of this incomparable monument of antiquity is, however, still an open question.

*History of the Acropolis until the Classical period*

The Acropolis crag measures 320 m (350 yd) from E to W and 156 m (170 yd) from N to S and rises to 156·2 m (512 ft) at its highest point. It falls steeply down on the N, E and S, so that since the earliest times the only access has been from the W.

In the Mycenaean period the "cyclopean" walls around the citadel closely followed the contours of the crag. In the N wall were two small gates leading down to the Klepsydra spring and the caves on the N face of the rock. The site of the later Old Temple of Athena was occupied by a royal palace, and there were dwelling houses to the E of the Erechtheion.

The Archaic period (7th and 6th c. B.C.) is represented by the remains of some ten buildings and parts of two temples.

All the buildings of the Archaic period were destroyed by the Persians in 480 B.C. During the reconstruction, which was begun immediately afterwards, Themistocles re-used column drums and fragments of entablature from the destroyed

*The Acropolis: a royal citadel which became a precinct of the gods*

buildings, still to be seen in the N wall. Later, after 467 B.C., the S side of the defences was altered by Kimon, who built the straight length of wall which still exists. Inside the Themistoclean N wall and Kimon's S wall the ground surface was built up, using the remains of buildings and sculpture which had been destroyed or damaged by the Persians. In this "Persian rubble" excavations in 1885–6 brought to light numerous pieces of sculpture and architectural fragments which are now among the treasures of the Acropolis Museum.

Within the extended area of Kimon's stronghold Pericles carried out his great programme of building and rebuilding:

in 447–438 B.C. the Parthenon;

in 437–432 B.C. the Propylaia;

in 432–421 B.C. the temple of Athena Nike;

in 421–406 B.C. the Erechtheion.

The only remains dating from a later period are those of a circular temple dedicated to Rome and Augustus (early Imperial period) outside the E end of the Parthenon.


## Agrippa, Monument of

On the way up from the Beulé Gate to the Propylaia, immediately below the Pinakotheke, is the tall rectangular plinth, in two colours of marble, of a monument built in the 2nd c. B.C. for a benefactor of Athens, perhaps a king of Pergamon. It is named after Marcus Agrippa, Augustus's son-in-law, whose quadriga (four-horse chariot) was set up on the base in 27 B.C.

## Arrhephoroi, House of

This house, a rectangular structure built against the N wall of the Acropolis with a porch and a courtyard to the left, was occupied by four girls between the ages of seven and eleven from the noblest families in Athens who assisted the priestess of Athena in serving the goddess. One of their duties was to make the new peplos worn by Athena at each four-yearly celebration of the Panathenaic festival (see Agora, Panathenaic Way).

From the courtyard a flight of steps led down through a gate in the outer wall of the Acropolis and a rock-cut passage to the sanctuary of Eros and the Cave of Aglauros, from which the Arrhephoroi had to fetch some secret cult objects (hence their name, "bearers of holy things").

A structure farther to the W along the N wall is believed to have been the house of the priestess of Appollo.

## Athena, Old Temple of

The Old Temple of Athena, also known as the Hekatompedon because its cella measured 32·8 by 16·4 m (100 by 50 ft), was built in the early 6th c. B.C. within the precincts of the Mycenaean royal palace of the 14th c. B.C. (now represented only by two column bases from its megaron, protected by gratings). The cella had no surrounding colonnade. The great pediment of poros limestone in the Acropolis Museum (Rooms II and III, see entry) probably came from this temple; it depicts in the centre bulls being attacked by lions, on the left Herakles and Triton, on the right a monster with three bodies (Nereus?). Around 525 B.C. Peisistratos built a temple with a colonnade of 6 by 12 columns, either a reconstruction of the Hekatompedon or an entirely new structure. In the pediment figures, depicting Athena in a fight with giants, marble was used for the first time on the Acropolis (see Acropolis Museum, Room V). This "Old Temple" superseded the Hekatompedon as the sanctuary of Athena Polias and took over the old wooden cult image of the goddess.

The temple was destroyed by the Persians in 480 B.C. together with all the other buildings of the Archaic period. In 406 B.C. the remains were razed to the ground after the transfer of the cult image to the new temple of Athena in the eastern part of the Erechtheion.

The foundations of the temple were brought to light in the 19th c.; they can be seen immediately S of the Erechtheion.

## Athena Hygieia, Sanctuary of

Among the many sanctuaries which lay within the walls of the Acropolis and have left traces in the limestone of the crag, was one sacred to Athena Hygieia. Beside the southern column of the E portico of the Propylaia is the semicircular base which once supported a bronze statue of the goddess. Opposite it is the square foundation of the altar.

*Temple of Athena Nike* ▶

## Athena Nike, Temple of

There was an ancient sanctuary dedicated to Athena as the bringer of victory (*nike*) on the spur of rock on the S side of the Propylaia – a rocky platform which lay outside the Mycenaean walls and served in Mycenaean times as a bastion protecting the entrance to the citadel.

The 6th c. structures were destroyed by the Persians in 480 B.C., but remains can be seen through openings in the facing applied to the rock in the classical period and on the floor of the temple. The temple was built in 432–421, after the completion of the Parthenon and the Propylaia. It has four Ionic columns at the N and S ends. The form of the column bases and capitals was already old-fashioned at the time of erection, leading Carpenter to suggest that after the end of the Periclean period the earlier design by Kallikrates was used (photograph, p. 33).

In Turkish times (1686) the temple was thrown down to use the bastion as an artillery position, from which Ludwig Ross disengaged it in 1836. Re-erected at that time, and again after consolidation work between 1936 and 1940, it is the daintiest and most elegant building on the Acropolis. Its Ionic forms contrast with the Doric massiveness of the Propylaia and with the ancient masonry of the "Pelasgian" (i.e. Mycenaean) defensive walls which can be seen to the E.

The Acropolis Museum (see entry) contains the balustrade from the temple platform, with relief figures of Athena and several representations of Nike (Victory).

## Athena Promachos, Statue of

Exactly in the axis of the central gate of the Propylaia stood a bronze statue of Athena Promachos (the "Champion"), a famous work by Phidias which stood 9 m (30 ft) high. The statue was later taken to Constantinople, and was destroyed during the Crusaders' siege of the city in 1203. The goddess, whose lance was visible from a great distance, stood on a marble base, parts of which, with an unusually large "egg-and-dart" moulding, are still *in situ*.

## Belvedere

This terrace at the NE corner of the Acropolis was laid out for the royal family in the 19th c., and affords a good view of the city looking towards Sýntagma Square (see entry) and the Old Palace.

## Beulé Gate

The Acropolis is entered by the Beulé Gate (named after the 19th c. French archaeologist who discovered it), below the W side of the Propylaia, which was the real entrance; admission tickets are sold here. The gate was built of material from the monument of Nikias and other structures destroyed in the Herulian raid of A.D. 267. With its two flanking towers, it lay on the axis of symmetry of the Propylaia, with which it was linked by a broad marble staircase built in the reign of the Emperor

*The sanctuary of Artemis Brauronia on the Acropolis*

Septimius Severus; part of the lower section of the staircase still survives.

## Brauronion

In the 6th c. B.C. Peisistratos brought the cult of Artemis to Athens from his home town of Brauron, and a sanctuary dedicated to this Artemis Brauronia was built in the SW part of the Acropolis, within the Propylaia and the "Pelasgian" wall. The altar and the cult statue, by Praxiteles, stood in an open courtyard with colonnades on the S and E sides. The sanctuary was given its final form by Mnesikles when built the Propylaia.

## Chalkotheke

About 450 B.C. a hall was built immediately adjoining the Brauronion for the safe keeping of bronze votive offerings and weapons, and after 432 a colonnade was built along the N wall. Adjoining this was a flight of steps hewn from the rock leading up to the Parthenon, originally decked with numerous votive offerings, including a representation of the Trojan Horse.

## Erechtheion

The Erechtheion, built between 421 and 395 B.C. and thus the youngest feature of the Acropolis in its classical form, incorporates a number of very ancient sanctuaries, and its complicated ground plan reflects the need to take account of these earlier structures.

The eastern part was occupied by the temple of Athena Polias, patron of the city, with the ancient and much venerated wooden cult figure (*xoanon*) which had previously stood in the Old Temple of Athena, no doubt perpetuating cult traditions going back to the palace which occupied the site in Mycenaean times.

In the western part of the Erechtheion were the tombs of king Erechtheus, who gave his name to the whole structure, and Kekrops, the mythical founder of the Athenian royal line. The tomb of Kekrops lay under the Porch of the Caryatids which projects on the S side of the Erechtheion, its entablature borne by six figures of maidens in place of columns.

On the N side is another cult feature. An opening in the floor affords a view of the rock in which the ancient Athenians saw the trident wielded by Poseidon when contending with Athena for possession of Attica.

The E and N porticos each had six Ionic columns, though the E portico now lacks one of its columns, which Lord Elgin carried off to London together with one of the caryatids and the rest of the "Elgin marbles".

The doorway leading from the N portico into the interior of the temple is a masterpiece of rich and delicate ornament. On the outer side of the cella wall, above elegant palmette ornament, is a frieze of grey Eleusinian marble on which were set white marble figures (originals in Acropolis Museum – see entry).

The building was altered during the Roman period, in particular the W side, which then received its two-storey form. It suffered further alterations in the 7th c., when it became a Christian church. In 1463 the Turkish commandant of the fortress used it for the accommodation of his harem. The result of these changes was that the interior lost its original division into the temple of Athena Polias to the E and the western part with the tomb of Erechtheus. Most of the exterior, with its delicate Ionic ornament, has survived.

From the N portico a side doorway leads into the adjoining cult precinct of the Pandroseion (see below), which in turn is adjoined on the S by the foundation walls of the Old Temple of Athena, lying under the Porch of the Caryatids.

To the E of the Erechtheion stood the altar belonging to this earlier temple.

The Erechtheion is at present being taken down in order to consolidate and re-erect the structure in accordance with the best conservational practice. The caryatids are temporarily housed in the Acropolis Museum (see entry).

## Eros and Aphrodite, Sanctuary of

Numerous votive tablets found in caves on the northern face of the Acropolis indicate that there was a sanctuary of Eros and

*The Erechtheion: general view*

Aphrodite here. In this area (below the Erechtheion to the NE, outside the walls) stood the "temple of Aphrodite in the gardens" mentioned by Pausanias – to be distinguished from a temple of the same name, but probably of later date, on the Ilissos. This temple could be reached from the Acropolis by a flight of steps still visible NE of the Erechtheion.

## Klepsydra

The Klepsydra spring, which, from the earliest times, supplied the Acropolis with water is at the W end of the northern face of the Acropolis. A rock-cut staircase beginning at the Beulé Gate, now walled up, gave access to the spring, which lies below the caves of Appollo and Pan. A well-house was built after the Persian wars.

## Pandroseion

In the obtuse angle between the Erechtheion and the Old Temple of Athena is the Pandroseion, a shrine named after Pandrosos, daughter of the first king of Athens, Kekrops, and sister of Herse and Aglauros, to whom one of the sacred caves on the N side of the Acropolis was dedicated (see Cave of Aglauros). The sanctuary was a rectangular courtyard enclosed by walls in which stood an altar of Zeus Herkeios (protector of the hearth) and no doubt also a small temple of Pandrosos. It was probably here too that the sacred snakes of the Acropolis

37

were kept. At the SE corner was an access to the tomb of Kekrops. Here too grew the sacred olive-tree presented to the city by Athena after her victory over Poseidon in the contest for the land of Attica. Herodotus (VIII, 55) tells us that on the day after the destruction of the Acropolis by the Persians in 480 B.C. a fresh shoot a cubit long had sprung from the trunk of the burned tree, giving an assurance of the continued survival of Athens. The memory of this olive-tree is perpetuated by a new tree planted here in modern times.

# Parthenon

This temple of Athena the Virgin (Athena Parthenos), built between 447 and 338 (the figures in the pediments being completed in 432), is the masterpiece of the architect Iktinos and the great sculptor Phidias, who was entrusted by Pericles with the general direction of the building operations on the Acropolis. The new Parthenon they built, however, was based on an earlier building on the same site.

Building history

On the basis of research by Hill, Dinsmoor and Carpenter the history of the building of the Parthenon can be summarised as follows:

490 B.C. (or soon afterwards): The foundations of the first Parthenon, consisting of 22 courses of masonry standing up to 10·75 m (35 ft) high, were constructed, with 6 columns at the ends and 16 along the sides. At the time of the Persian attack in 480 it was still unfinished. The column drums were damaged in the burning of the Acropolis and were built into the Themistoclean N wall.

468 B.C.: Kimon continued the construction of the temple, the "Pre-Parthenon", the architect being Kallikrates. On Kimon's death (450 B.C.) work was suspended.

447 B.C.: Under Pericles, the new leader of Athens, the erection of the Parthenon proper began. Kallikrates was replaced by Iktinos, who used the building materials aready available. The foundations were now adjusted to the new and wider ground plan. (On the S side of the Parthenon can be seen the older foundations, projecting farther at the E end; the widening can also be observed in the northern part of the foundations at the W end.)

The substructure (crepidoma) of the new temple consisted of 3 steps each 52 cm (20 in.) high. There were now 8 columns at the ends and 17 along the sides, compared with the previous 6 and 16. The Doric columns are 10·43 m (34 ft) high, with a diameter of 1·90 m (6 ft 3 in.) at the foot and 1·48 m (4 ft 10 in.) at the top, and have 20 flutings. Note the entasis (swelling) of the columns and the curvature of the crepidoma, rising towards the middle (best seen on the top step, the stylobate). These optical refinements, like the slight inward inclination of the columns, with the corner columns leaning diagonally inward, were designed to relieve the rigidity and solidity of the building and create an effect of organic structure.

The roof was covered with marble tiles. The lions' heads at the eaves were solid and cannot therefore have been designed as water-spouts, in accordance with the usual practice; there were run-offs for rainwater at the four corners of the roof. The holes on the architrave of the E end mark the position of the

*The Parthenon*

pegs on which were hung the shields captured by Alexander the Great in the battle of the Granikos (334 B.C.) and dedicated by him to Athena.

The interior of the Parthenon – now closed to visitors – is in two parts. At the W end is a rear chamber (opisthodomos), with traces of painting dating from the use of the Parthenon as a Christian church dedicated to the Virgin, leading into the temple proper, the roof of which was borne on four Ionic columns. This probably served as the state treasury.

Interior

At the E end is the pronaos, giving access to the chamber which contained the chryselephantine (gold and ivory) statue of Athena, a cult image known to us only from descriptions and later copies. It was supported by a massive post, the hole for which can be seen in the floor of the cella.

The statue, completed in 438 B.C., was one of Phidias' most renowned works, ranking with the figure of Athena Promachos on the Acropolis and that of Zeus in the Temple of Zeus at Olympia. It stood 12 m (39 ft) high, and the gold used in the dress and ornaments is said to have weighed about a ton; the gold was detachable, and could thus be removed to check the weight. The face and hands were of ivory. Like the Athena Promachos, the statue was carried off to Constantinople and was destroyed there in 1203.

Marks on the floor indicate that there was a two-storey colonnade on both sides and to the rear of the statue. Iktinos thus achieved a wholly new conception of the interior of a temple, which was no longer merely designed as a chamber to house the cult image. It has been supposed that the widening of the ground plan of the temple from six to eight columns was made necessary by this new conception, so that here, for the first time in a Greek temple, the interior chamber with the cult statue determined the whole plan of the structure.

Exterior

Sculpture

No less celebrated than the cult statue was the sculpture on the exterior of the Parthenon – the two pediments, the Doric metopes and the Ionic frieze around the upper part of the cella wall. It is characteristic of the Parthenon that an Ionic feature of this kind was used in a Doric temple, reflecting a firm intention to link the two orders together: Periclean Athens was to be the point of crystallisation of Doric as well as Ionic Hellenism.

Some of the sculpture is still *in situ*, and there is some in the Acropolis Museum (see entry). There is also some in the Louvre in Paris, but most of it is in the British Museum, having been transported to London by Lord Elgin in 1801.

Pediments

The pediments, completed in 432 B.C., depict the birth of Athena from the head of Zeus (E end) and the conflict between Athena and Poseidon for the land of Attica (W end). The E pediment now contains copies of Dionysos (on left) and the heads of the sun god's horses and the moon goddess (at both corners). The W pediment has the figure of king Kekrops with one of his daughters (original).

Doric frieze

The 92 metopes of the Doric frieze depicted a fight with giants (E), a fight with centaurs (S: the best preserved), a fight with Persians or with Amazons (W) and the Trojan War (N).

Ionic frieze

The Ionic frieze on the outer wall of the cella, 1·05 m (3 ft 5 in.) high and 160 m (525 ft) long, is not devoted to mythical or historical subjects like the pediments and metopes but reflects the life of Athens in the Classical period. It depicts the Panathenaic festival, held every four years, when a great procession made its way from the Gymnasion at the Dipylon, by way of the Agora, to the Acropolis (see Agora, Panathenaic Way). The procession begins at the SW corner, runs to the left along the W end, where the slabs bearing the reliefs are still *in situ* (with a recently erected protective roof), and then continues along the N side to the E end, where it meets the other half of the procession running along the S side. The object of the procession was to present a new peplos to the goddess Athena, who was depicted on the E end. The frieze is a masterly representation of the people of Athens playing their part in this great national religious occasion, with men, women, riders, sacrificial animals and officials, subtly organised in rhythmic groups, all moving towards their goal at a stately pace or in rapid advance.

Later history

The Parthenon suffered considerable damage when in the 5th c., after serving as a temple for some 900 years, it was transformed into a Christian chuch dedicated to the Virgin. Among the changes then made was the construction of an apse, involving the destruction of the central group on the E pediment. The disfigurement of many of the metopes, on the

*Fight with a centaur (SW metope of Parthenon)*

basis of their "pagan" character, is no doubt also to be dated to the Christian period.

The Parthenon remained in use as a church for some 950 years before becoming a Turkish mosque in 1456. The only changes made by the Turks were the removal of the Christian additions and the construction of a minaret at the SW corner – 231 years later a Venetian grenade blew up the powder magazine which the Turks had installed in the Parthenon, and the building which had stood for more than 2100 years was destroyed. A small mosque was later built in the ruins. In the 19th c. this was removed, as were all the other Turkish and Crusader structures on the Acropolis, leaving the Parthenon a ruin but a purely Greek one.

## Philhellenes, Monument to

Going up towards the Acropolis from Dionysíou Areopagítou Street (where the tourist buses stop), not on the broad paved way but on the footpath beside the Odeion of Herodes Atticus, we see on the left a triangular marble pillar with an inscription commemorating the French general Baron Nicolas Favier (1782–1855) and Major Frank Robert, who defended the Acropolis against the Turks in 1826.

## Propylaia

The Propylaia were built by Mnesikles in 437–432 B.C. as a monumental tripartite entrance to the Acropolis, taking the

*The Propylaia, looking towards the doorways in the central structure*

place of a 6th c. propylon of which traces can still be seen. On the native rock is set a flight of marble steps, the lowest step of grey Eleusinian marble, the others of light-coloured Pentelic marble. The central part of the structure is a vestibule with a rear wall containing five gateways, which increase in width and height from the sides to the centre. The lintel of the central doorway has an additional metope – a solution adopted here for the first time which later became common.

To the W is a deep portico, with a central doorway framed in 2 × 3 Ionic columns. Along the front of this portico are six Doric columns which originally supported the pediment. Compared with this imposing entrance the E portico, also with Doric columns but shorter and lower, appears small and modest when seen from the higher part of the Acropolis, subordinating itself to the more important cult buildings. Adjoining the W portico are other structures, including the Pinakotheke, which contained a collection of paintings. To the W of this is a plinth of the 2nd c. B.C. which was later occupied by a monument to Agrippa.

On the S side a building similar to the Pinakotheke was planned, but this bold plan had to be modified to take account of the old sanctuary of Athena Nike, and in Mnesikles' hands it became merely a narrow vestibule leading to the temple of Nike.

From the 13th c. onwards the Propylaia served as the residence of rulers and military commanders and as defensive fortifications, and were much altered and disfigured. The holes which supported beams bearing intermediate floors can still be seen. The central structure was destroyed between 1640 and

1656 by the explosion of an ammunition store. A bastion which was later built between the S wing and the platform bearing the temple of Athena Nike was removed in 1836, and the Frankish Tower, built in the 14th c. by the Florentine Duke of Athens, Nerio Acciaiuoli, was pulled down by Schliemann in 1875 at his own expense. Extensive restoration works began in 1909.

## Rome and Augustus, Temple of

In 27 B.C. the Romans built, outside the E end of the Parthenon and on its central axis, a circular temple on a square tufa substructure. The roof was borne by nine Ionic columns, with capitals painstakingly modelled on those of the Erechtheion. The temple contained statues of Rome and Augustus, to whom it was dedicated.

## Sacred caves

On the northern slopes of the Acropolis are a number of caves which in ancient times were dedicated to the cult of the gods. Near the W end, close together, are threee such caves, two of them sacred to Apollo, the third to Pan. They were originally accessible from the Acropolis by a flight of steps.

The most easterly of the three, lying below the House of the Arrhephoroi, is the Cave of Aglauros, in which sacred festivals were celebrated with music and dancing. Here, too, the ephebes swore their oath. Cave of Aglauros

The cave is named after Aglauros, one of the three daughters of Kekrops. She and her sister Herse opened a casket which had been entrusted to them by Athena, although they had been forbidden to tamper with it: whereupon they lost their reason and sprang to their deaths from the summit of the Acropolis. The third of the sisters, Pandrosos, escaped this fate and has a sanctuary dedicated to her on the Acropolis (see Pandroseion, above).

The most westerly of the caves was sacred to Apollo Hypoakraios. The site of the altar was found outside the entrance, and in the walls of the cave are small niches with votive inscriptions. Cave of Apollo Hypoakraios

A little way E is another cave which was also dedicated to Apollo. Here he seduced Kreousa, who later exposed her son Ion in the cave.

In the eastern part of this cave a chapel dedicated to St Athanasius was installed in Christian times.

The largest cave was sacred to the old shepherd god Pan, who was particularly honoured in Athens after the Persian wars, since the Athenian victory of Marathon (490 B.C.) was attributed to his aid. Cave of Pan

## Zeus Polieus, Sanctuary of

NE of the Parthenon and N of the temple of Rome and Augustus is the highest point on the Acropolis, which was occupied by the sanctuary of Zeus Polieus, an open cult precinct (*temenos*) containing an altar and a stable for the sacrificial animals (Boukoleion). The only remains of the sanctuary are cuttings in the rock.

---

## **Acropolis Museum** C2/3

---

**Electric Railway**
Theseion station

**Bus**
16

**Opening times**
Mon.–Sat. 9 a.m.–6.30 p.m.
Sun. 10 a.m.–4.30 p.m.

The Acropolis Museum, containing one of the most valuable collections of Greek art in existence, was built in 1949–53 at the SE corner of the Acropolis, lying so low that it does not obtrude. The rooms to the left contain material of the Archaic period (6th c. B.C.) which formed part of the "Persian rubble" and was recovered during excavations by Panayiotis Kavvadias in 1885–6: pediments from temples and treasuries, votive statues and (in the rooms to the right) marble figures from the pediment of the Old Temple of Athena (Rooms I–V). In the other rooms to the right (VI–XI) is sculpture of the Classical period (5th c.).

The Vestibule is dominated by a large owl, the emblem of Athena (No. 1347: early 5th c. B.C.). Here, too, is a marble statue of Athena, "Athena Propylaia" (No. 1336: end of 5th c.); a marble base with a relief of soldiers dancing (No. 1338: 4th c. B.C.); and a marble funerary lekythos (No. 6407: end of 4th c.). The caryatids from the Erechtheion are temporarily housed in a room to the right.

Room I (early 6th c. B.C.): To the left is a pediment group in painted poros limestone depicting Herakles fighting the Lernaean hydra (No. 1: *c.* 600 B.C.).
Opposite the entrance is a lioness rending a young bull, from a large poros pediment (No. 4: *c.* 490 B.C.); to the right is a Gorgon (No. 701: beginning of 6th c. B.C.).

Room II: Introduction of Herakles to Olympus (on left, No. 9/55: *c.* 580 B.C.).
The right-hand half of the "Red Pediment", depicting Herakles and Triton (No. 2: *c.* 560 B.C.).
The "Olive-tree Pediment", probably portraying the myth of Troilos, with a representation of a temple and a girl carrying water (No. 52: *c.* 570 B.C.).
Two sections of a poros pediment, probably from the old Temple of Athena: to the left Harakles and Triton, to the right a three-bodied monster, now believed to be Nereus (No. 35: 580–570 B.C.). The central section of the pediment was probably the group of two lions rending a bull displayed in Room III (No. 3).
Here, too, are the famous Moschoporos ("Calf-Bearer") of Hymettian marble, a votive offering by Rhombos (No. 624: *c.* 570 B.C.), and the earliest of the korai, the figures of girls which were set up in large numbers on the Acropolis as votive offerings to Athena; in one hand this Attic work holds a pomegranate, in the other a garland (No. 593: beginning of 6th c. B.C.).

Room III: Central section of a pediment group (cf. Room II) and the torsos of two other korai, probably from Naxos or Samos (Nos. 619 and 677: 580–550 B.C.).

*Figure of a hound by Phaidimos (c. 520 B.C.) from the Brauronion*

Room IV contains a large number of master works. First come four or perhaps five works attributed to the same sculptor, Phaidimos. The earliest is the so-called Rampin Horseman, the head of which is a cast (original in the Louvre). Together with a second horseman preserved in fragments this formed the earliest known equestrian group in Greece. It is believed to represent either Hippias and Hipparchos, the sons of Peisistratos, or the Dioscuri (No. 590: *c.* 550 B.C.).

A famous mature work by the same sculptor is the "Peplos Kore", named after the Doric garment which she wears. A lion-head spout from the Old Temple of Athena (No. 61: *c.* 525 B.C.) and a hound from the Brauronion (No. 143: *c.* 520 B.C.) are also attributed to Phaidimos.

A figure of a horseman in Persian or Scythian costume probably represents Miltiades (No. 606: *c.* 520 B.C.).

In the rear part of Room IV are a group of korai, wearing the peplos or later the more elegant chiton, usually covered with the himation (cloak). As a rule one hand gathers in the maiden's garment while the other holds a votive offering. These figures, mostly life-size, stood in the open air, and many of them still preserve the fixing of the meniskos, an iron shield designed to protect them from bird droppings. The figures were originally painted, and some traces of colouring can still be seen, particularly on the garments.

First come a kore with a serious expression, wearing Ionic costume (No. 673: 520–510 B.C.), a graceful kore from Chios in an elegantly draped painted chiton (No. 675: *c.* 510 B.C.) and a very fine head (No. 643: *c.* 510 B.C.).

Then, in a wide semicircle, are (from left to right) a large kore from Chios (No. 682: *c.* 520 B.C.), a vigorous figure, probably from the Peloponnese (No. 684: *c.* 490 B.C.), the enigmatic "Sphinx-Eyed Kore" (No. 674: *c.* 500 B.C.) and a kore clad only in a chiton (No. 670: *c.* 510 B.C.).

A large and badly weathered seated figure of Athena (in the centre of the group) by Endoios (No. 625: *c.* 530 B.C.) is followed by the clothed figure of a youth (No. 633: end of 6th *c.* B.C.), a severe kore, the only one not girding her garment (No. 685: *c.* 500 B.C.), an almost unworn kore from the Ionian Islands (No. 680: *c.* 520 B.C.) and a large kore, also almost undamaged (No. 671: *c.* 520 B.C.).

Room V: The most notable item is the Kore of Antenor, 2 m (6 ft) high, standing on a base bearing the name of the donor, Nearchos, and the sculptor, Antenor, which probably does not belong to it (Nos. 681 and 681A: *c.* 525 B.C.).

The room is dominated by statues from the pediment of the Peisistratid Old Temple depicting Athena fighting giants (No. 631: *c.* 525 B.C.).

In the alcove to the left is a collection of pottery ranging in date from the Geometric to the late Classical period.

Room VI (early 5th c. B.C.): The earliest works belonging to this first stage of classical art date from before the Persian conquest (480 B.C.). This room contains work of this phase together with examples of the "Severe" style.

Among outstanding items are the "Sulky Kore" (Nos. 686 and 609: *c.* 490 B.C.), dedicated by Euthydikos; the "Kore of the Propylaia", set up shortly before the Persian attack (No. 688: *c.* 480 B.C.); a statue of Athena (No. 140: 480–470 B.C.); a relief figure of a potter (No. 1332: *c.* 500 B.C.); the head of a youth, from the workshop of Phidias (No. 699: 450–440 B.C.); and the forequarters of a horse, a noble work of 490–480 B.C. (No. 697).

Famous works of the early Classical period are the "Fair-Haired Youth", a figure of unusual melancholy beauty (No. 689: shortly before 480 B.C.); a relief of "Mourning Athena" (No. 695: 460–450 B.C.); and the oldest of the group, the figure of a boy ascribed to Kritios or his workshop (No. 698: 485 B.C.). The torso and head of this "Critian Boy" were found in 1865 and 1888. It is the earliest known figure in which the archaic posture with each leg bearing an equal weight gives place to the classical pose in which one leg bears the weight and the other hangs free. In this respect Kritios was a forerunner of the art of the Classical period.

The following rooms are devoted to the buildings of the Classical period on the Acropolis.

Room VII: Plaster reproductions of the Parthenon pediments, a metope from the S side (centaurs and Lapiths: No. 705), a torso of Poseidon from the W pediment (No. 885a) and two horses' heads from Poseidon's team (Nos. 882 and 884).

Room VIII: Large sections of the Parthenon frieze (160 m (525 ft) long, 1·05 m (3 ft 5 in.) high), depicting the great Panathenaic procession (see Agora, Panathenaic Way) and giving a vivid impression of life in Athens in the age of Pericles.

From the N frieze: horsemen, *apobatai* (who jump off and on moving chariots), marshals, musicians, youths, carrying hydrias and sacrificial animals. The last slab (No. 857) is undoubtedly the work of Phidias himself.

From the S frieze: horsemen.

From the E frieze: Poseidon, Apollo and Artemis, probably carved by Alkamenes, a pupil of Phidias.

On the projecting wall which divides the room into two are parts of the Erechtheion frieze, carved some decades after the Parthenon frieze (between 409 and 405 B.C.). The reconstruction shows the techniques used, the figures in light-coloured Pentelic marble being attached to the background of darker marble with metal pegs. The significance of the figures is unclear.

Finally there are a series of slabs from the parapet round the temple of Athena Nike (*c.* 410 B.C.). The reliefs, which originally decorated the outer side of the parapet, depict a seated Athena (No. 989) with a number of goddesses of victory, including the famous Nike loosing her sandal (No. 973).

Room IX: A large mask of a deity (No. 6461), a bas-relief of an Attic trireme (No. 1339) and – the most notable item – an idealised portrait of the young Alexander, probably carved by Leochares or Euphranor after Alexander's visit to Athens in 335 B.C. (No. 1331).

---

## * *Aegina (Aíyina)

---

This island in the Saronic Gulf is a popular resort of both Athenians and visitors from farther afield, combining the attractions of its scenery (cultivated fields, pistachio nuts and, further S, citrus fruits, macchia and forests) with its great tourist sight, the Temple of Aphaia, and its extensive beaches and facilities for all kinds of water sports. From Aegina, too, there are boat services to the islands of Poros, Hydra and Spetsai.

The earliest settlement of the island dates back to the 4th millennium B.C., and by around 2500 B.C. there was a fortified trading post on the W coast carrying on trade with the mainland, the Cyclades and Crete. Dorian immigrants who arrived about 1000 B.C. continued this tradition, and by the 7th c. B.C. the island's trading connections extended as far as Egypt and Spain. About 650 B.C. Aegina minted the first coins in Europe. In the 5th c. B.C. there was increasing conflict with Athens, which in 459 B.C. compelled the island to surrender and destroyed its economic power.

The island recovered a measure of importance for a brief period in 1826, when it became the seat of the first Greek government headed by Kapodistrias. A year later, however, the seat of government was transferred to Nauplia.

**Landing-stages**
Aíyina Town, Ayía Marína

**Departure**
Piraeus

## Aíyina Town

The island's capital, Aíyina, has a population of 6100. The neo-classical style of its architecture recalls its brief period of importance as the seat of the Greek government in 1826.

*Harbour, Aegina*

On the N breakwater of the harbour (which was the commercial harbour of the ancient city) is a chapel dedicated to St Nicholas, and a cathedral on the quay.

**Excavations of the ancient city**

**Opening times**
Daily from 8 a.m. to sunset

Just to the N was the ancient naval harbour, and here, too, was the site of the ancient city, which has recently been under excavation by German archaeologists.

The dominant feature of the excavation site is a temple of Apollo, built in the 5th c. B.C. over an earlier (7th c.) sanctuary. One column of the temple is still *in situ*.

W of the temple excavation has brought to light Bronze Age structures and a Roman fountain. To the SE of the temple was found a structure of the 6th c B.C., probably the Aiakeion, the funerary monument of Aegina's mythical first king Aiakos.

**Archaeological Museum**

**Opening times**
Mon.–Sat. 8 a.m.–1 p.m. and 3–6 p.m.
Sun. 10 a.m.–4.50 p.m.

The Museum adjoins the Mitrópolis (Cathedral) and, like it, dates from the 19th c. Its three rooms contain material dating back to about 2500 B.C.

Centre room: Terracotta frieze from the old Temple of Aphaia (580 B.C.) and fragments from the Late Archaic temple; pottery from Egypt and Asia Minor; finds from the Temple of Apollo, oil lamps.

Left-hand room: Neolithic and later pottery – Minoan, Geometric, Orientalising, black-figure and red-figure vases, including an Attic vase with Odysseus and Polyphemos (*c.* 600 B.C.).

Right-hand room: Marble sphinx (in centre of room), funerary monuments ranging in date from the Classical period to Roman times.

## Omorphi Ekklisía

This tiny church, the "Beautiful Church", lies to the E of the town. 1 km (¾ mile) from the town centre, at the Ayii Asómati sign, a road branches off on the left, and from this another road goes off on the left to the church. Dedicated to the two SS. Theodore, it was built in *c.* 1282 by the Sagomalas family of Athens, as an inscription over the doorway records. Stone from ancient buildings was re-used in its construction.

The barrel-vaulted interior is decorated with frescoes, probably rather younger than the church itself. In the apse is a figure of the Mother of God enthroned (Theotokos Platytéra). The cycle of church festivals begins on the S side of the church, with a representation of the Nativity, and continues on the N side and the W end.

## Ayía Marína

Ayía Marína is a bay on the E side of the island in which a hotel settlement, much frequented by both local people and visitors, has developed in recent years. Cruise parties to visit Aphaia disembark here.

## Ayía Triáda

7·5 km (4½ miles) from the town of Aíyina on the road to Paleochóra are St Catherine's monastery and the nunnery of Ayía Triáda (the Trinity). Ayía Triáda is also known as Ayios Nektários, after the newest saint of the Greek Orthodox Church, who died in 1920. His marble sarcophagus, in a small chapel, attracts large numbers of pilgrims.

## Oros

The Oros ("Mountain"), also known as Profítis Ilías, is the island's highest point (524 m – 1719 ft). It can be climbed by taking a bus from Aíyina to the little village of Marathón, from which it is an hour and a half's walk to the summit. On top of the hill was a settlement, dating from about the 13th c. B.C., in which Zeus Hellanios was worshipped. The remains of a semicircular wall mark the site of his temple; the position of the altar is now occupied by a chapel dedicated to the Prophet Elijah (Profítis Ilías).

## Paleochóra

The town of Paleochóra, capital of the island in the Middle Ages, is reached from Aíyina by taking the Ayía Marína road as far as the nunnery of Ayía Triáda (7·5 km – 4½ miles) and then following a road to the left which leads to a modern church. From here a path on the right ascends to the hill on which Paleochóra lies.

Paleochóra (the "Old Village") was founded in the 9th c., when the coastal villages were abandoned because of the danger of pirate raids and the population withdrew into the interior. The town flourished until 1654, when it was besieged and destroyed by the Venetians. It was finally abandoned after 1800, when the present town of Aíyina was founded on the coast. The houses, some 400 in number, fell into ruin, but 28 of the town's churches survived – modest buildings mostly dating from the 13th and 14th c. A few of the churches have been restored in recent years.

Services are still held here on the festivals of the Mother of God, but otherwise the town is deserted.

**Ayios Dionýsios**

This chapel, near the Episkopí church (see below), is dedicated to St Dionysios of Zakynthos, who lived here as a hermit for some time.

**Ayios Yeóryios Katholikós**

This church, situated on the slopes of the hill, has an inscription of 1533 above the doorway, but is probably earlier. The lie of the land made it impossible to give the church the canonical E–W orientation, and it is therefore asymmetrical in plan. It has a stone iconostasis.

**Ayios Yeóryios and Ayios Dimítrios**

This double chapel, built by the Venetians, stands on the summit of the hill near the ruins of a castle.

**Ayios Ioánnis o Theológos**

This 14th c. church, on a Greek cross plan, has a blue dome. It contains a number of frescoes (St George, and the Virgin Mary).

**Ayios Nikólaos**

This church, near SS. George and Demetrius, is the oldest in Paleochóra (13th c.). It contains interesting frescoes (Mother of God in the dome of the apse, St George and other saints) and a stone iconostasis.

**Episkopí**

This church, once the seat of a bishop, lies near the chapel of St Dionysios below the summit of the hill. Material from ancient buildings was re-used in its construction. It is a domed church, with an aisle on the S side of the nave. Two of the columns have ancient capitals. There is a 16th c. icon of the Panayía (the Mother of God) on the iconostasis, and the church also has 17th c. frescoes.

**Zoodóchos Piyí**

This church, dedicated to the Virgin Mary as the "Life-Giving Spring", lies above the ruined monastery of Ayía Kyriakí. It contains 17th c. frescoes.

# Panayía Chrysoleóntissa

This nunnery, dedicated to the most holy Virgin of the Golden Lion, lies in a valley on the N side of the Oros. It can be reached by walking down from the hill or from the road from Aíyina to the Temple of Aphaia, turning off below the nunnery of Ayía Triáda (40 minutes' walk).

The nunnery, enclosed within massive walls, dates from about 1600 and was enlarged in 1806. The church has an icon of the Mother of God and a beautifully carved iconostasis with Old Testament scenes.

*Temple of Aphaia, Aegina* ▶

## Temple of Aphaia

The Temple of Aphaia, 12 km (7½ miles) from the town of Aíyina, dominates the E coast of the island. The site was first excavated in 1811 by three architects (C. Haller, von Hallerstein and Cockerell), who discovered 17 marble figures from the pediments. These were acquired by Crown Prince Ludwig of Bavaria, who had them restored by the Danish sculptor Thorvaldsen in Rome in 1815–17 and then, in 1828, sent them to Munich, where they can be seen in the Glyptothek.

The first systematic excavations, carried out by A. Furtwängler in 1901, brought to light a dedicatory inscription to Aphaia, goddess of fertility. The inscription came from an earlier building of about 580 B.C. which gave place to the present temple around 510. At that time Athena apparently joined Aphaia as joint patroness of the temple.

The sacred precinct is entered from the S. After passing the propylon, to the right of which are priests' quarters, we come to the main complex consisting of the temple, the altar to the E of the temple and a ramp running between the two.

The Doric temple, "the most polished building of the late Archaic period" (Gruben), is built of limestone, which was originally faced with stucco. The pediment figures, depicting the Trojan War, and the roof were of marble. Well preserved and extensively restored, the temple is of imposing effect. The cella, with three aisles separated by two-tiered rows of columns, is surrounded by a colonnade of 6×12 columns. The cult image stood between the last-but-one pair of columns in the cella. At the W end of the temple, where further excavations are in progress, it is possible to look down into the foundations of the building. The fallen columns were re-erected in 1956–60, but lightning has caused damage to the SW corner.

From the temple there are fine views of much of the island, extending as far as the Oros which dominates the landscape. In clear weather it is possible to see the Acropolis in Athens.

---

## ** Agorá                                                              C2

**Situation**
Between Leofóros Apostólou
Pávlou and Adrianoú

**Electric Railway**
Theseion station

**Buses**
10, 72, 93/10

**Opening times**
Mon. and Wed.–Sat. 8 a.m.–
8 p.m.
Sun. 10 a.m.–4.30 p.m.

**Closed**
Tues.

In the area N of the Acropolis (see entry) there are three large open areas – the Agora, the principal market-place of ancient Athens, the Roman Agora (see entry) and the Library of Hadrian (see entry).

A good general impression of the Agora can be obtained from four viewpoints: the N wall of the Acropolis, the Areopagos, the road which runs E from the Areopagos along the N side of the Acropolis, and the road along the N side of the Areopagos. The detailed layout of the Agora can best be appreciated by entering the site at the N gate, off Adrianoú Street (near the church of St Philip), and consulting the plan displayed just inside the entrance.

The Agora was excavated by American archaeologists in 1931–41 and 1946–60 after the demolition of a whole district of the city which had grown up since the 11th c., and the remains have been incorporated in an attractive park. Since 1970 further excavations have been carried out N of the Piraeus railway, which previously formed the boundary of the excavation site, and to the E of the Agora, where, under a modern road, excavation has brought to light the ancient road linking the Agora with the Roman market, together with the buildings flanking the road.

From the Mycenaean period until the end of the 7th c. B.C. this was a cemetery area. It began to be used as an agora during the early 6th c., in the time of Solon, and the oldest buildings were erected at the W end of the site, under the Agora Hill. Thereafter it remained for many centuries the centre of the city's public life, each century erecting new buildings, frequently at the expense of earlier ones.

At the W end of the Agora, between the Metroon and the Stoa of Zeus at the foot of the Agora Hill, are the foundations of the temple of Apollo Patroos, built in the 4th c. B.C. over the remains of buildings destroyed in the Persian wars and dedicated to Apollo as the father of Ion and thus the forefather of the Ionians. The cult image of Apollo and Euphranor from the temple is now in the Stoas of Attalos. In an annex to the temple the earliest register of the population of Athens was kept.

Temple of Apollo Patroos

Immediately N are the foundations of a small sanctuary of Zeus Phratrios and Athena Phratria, also dating from the 4th c. B.C.

The most prominent feature on the E side of the Agora is the 116 m (380 ft) long Stoa of Attalos, built by king Attalos II of Pergamon (160–139 B.C.), brother and successor to Eumenes II, who built the Stoa of Eumenes on the S side of the Acropolis. The stoa was (and is, since the faithful reconstruction of the original building in 1953–6) two-storeyed, with Doric columns fronting the lower floor and Ionic columns on the upper floor. The stoa proper, which is backed by a series of rectangular rooms (originally 21), is divided by Ionic columns into two aisles. The reconstruction has restored the impressive spatial effect of the long pillared hall. In ancient times the stoa was occupied by offices and shops; it now houses the Agora Museum (see entry).

Stoa of Attalos

In front of the stoa, near the N end, are remains of a small hall and a circular fountain-house. Half-way along are an orator's rostrum (bema) and the base which bore a statue of Attalos.

The Temple of Ares stood in the northern part of the Agora; originally built on another site around 440 B.C., it was moved to its present position in the Augustan period. Although only scanty remains have survived, there is sufficient evidence to establish that this temple resembled the Temple of Hephaistos and was probably built by the same architect. The cult image of Ares, god of war, carved by Alkamenes, has been lost, but the excavators found a statue of Athena and a number of relief figures (from an interior frieze) which are now in the Agora Museum (see entry). Also in the museum is the central acroterion from the E front, representing Ares's sister Hebe. Outside the E front of the temple is the altar.

Temple of Ares

The Bouleuterion, meeting-place of the Council (Boule) of Athens, was built in 403 B.C. on the slope below the Temple of Hephaistos. A vestibule on the S side led into the main council chamber, with the semicircular rows of seats for the 500

Bouleuterion

members of the Council rising in tiers like the auditorium of a theatre. The building was destroyed by the Herulians in A.D. 267, but was rebuilt and remained in existence until about 400.

**Great Drain**

The Great Drain was constructed in the early 5th c. B.C. to channel the rainwater which flowed down from the Acropolis and Areopagos (see entries) into the Eridanos. From the SW end of the Agora it runs NE and then bears N, passing in front of the buildings on the W side of Agora. 1 m (3 ft 3 in.) wide and 1 m (3 ft 3 in.) deep, it is constructed of polygonal masonry.

At the point where the drain turns N and is joined by a subsidiary channel coming from the SE stands the Horos, or boundary stone of the Agora, which was set up around 500 B.C. to separate the public part of the Agora from the official buildings along the W side.

**Eleusinion**

On the E side of the Panathenaic Way (see below), which climbed up to the Acropolis, was a sanctuary of the Eleusinian divinities Demeter, Persephone and Triptolemos. It was smaller than the one in Eleusis, but large enough to accommodate a meeting of the Council of 500 on the day after the celebration of the mysteries.

In the centre of the precinct are the foundations of a temple, with an antechamber leading into the adyton (the "not to be entered" holy of holies). The temple, which stood on a high terrace, was extended southward in Roman times.

**Peribolos of Eponymous Heroes**

Opposite the Metroon (see below) is a long narrow rectangular base. On this there stood statues of the ten eponymous heroes who gave their names to the ten tribes (*phylai*) into which the population of Attica was divided. Here in ancient times new laws were made public.

**Statue of Hadrian**

Among the numerous monuments the bases of which have been preserved along the W side of the Agora was a statue of the Emperor Hadrian (117–138) erected in the 2nd c. A.D. This well-preserved figure is notable for the quality of the carving, particularly the richly decorated breastplate.

**Heliaia**

The Heliaia, a court established by Solon in the 6th c. B.C., had its meeting-place on the S side of the Agora. It was named after the sun god Helios because it held its sessions before sunrise. There are remains of a large rectangular structure, on the N side of which can be seen a klepsydra (water-clock) and, on the W side, a fountain-house with two wings meeting at right angles.

**Temple of Hephaistos**

From the Agora an attractive footpath runs past the Tholos (see below) up the Agora Hill (Kolonos Agoraios), on which stands the Temple of Hephaistos. The erroneous name of Theseion still stubbornly persists (and is perpetuated by the name of the nearby station on the Piraeus railway); but the actual situation of the real Theseion, in which the remains of the Attic hero Theseus were deposited after being brought back by Kimon from the island of Skyros in 475 B.C., remains unknown.

The Hephaisteion, lying near the smiths' and craftsmen's quarter of Athens, was dedicated to the divinities of the smiths and the arts, Hephaistos and Athena. It is one of the best preserved of surviving Greek temples, thanks to the conversion into a Christian church which saved it from destruction.

*Temple of Hephaistos on the Agora Hill*

This Doric temple, with the classical plan of 6×13 columns, was built about the same time as the Parthenon (see Acropolis) but is considerably smaller (columns 5·71 m (19 ft) high, Parthenon 10·43 m – 34 ft). It has, however, certain features (e.g. Ionic friezes instead of Doric triglyphs on the façades of the pronaos and opisthodomos) which appear to be modelled on the Parthenon. The explanation is that building began, probably under the direction of Kallikrates, before 449 B.C. but was suspended to allow concentration of effort on Pericles' great building programme on the Acropolis and resumed only during the Peace of Nikias (421–415 B.C.), after Pericles' death.

This late date explains the more recent aspect of the E end, with the entrance to the temple. Here the portico, the coffered ceiling of which is completely preserved, is three bays deep (compared with one and a half at the W end) and is tied in to the axis of the third column; the pronaos frieze is carried across to the N and S peristyles; and the metopes have carved decoration, while elsewhere they are plain. All these features are innovations which give greater emphasis to the E end, departing from the earlier principle of a balance between the two ends.

The damaged pronaos frieze depicts battle scenes, the W frieze fighting between Lapiths and centaurs (in the middle the invulnerable Lapith Kaineus being driven into the ground by centaurs).

In spite of its small size, the cella had columns round three sides framing the cult images of Hephaistos and Athena (by Alkamenes) which were set up in the temple about 420 B.C., this also in imitation of the Parthenon. The cella walls were roughened and covered with paintings.

When in the 5th c. the temple was converted into a Christian church, dedicated to St George, it became necessary to construct a chancel at the E end in place of the previous entrance. A new entrance (still preserved) was therefore broken through the W wall of the cella, and the old E entrance wall and the two columns of the pronaos were removed and replaced by an apse. At the same time the timber roof, normal in Greek temples, was replaced by the barrel-vaulting which still survives. Scanty remains of painting, dating from the period of use as a church, can be seen on the N external wall.

When King Otto entered the new capital of Greece in 1834, a solemn service was held in St George's Church (depicted in a painting by Peter von Hess in the Neue Pinakothek, Munich). Thereafter it became a museum and continued to serve that purpose into the present century.

Metroon

The remains of the Metroon, a sanctuary of the Mother of the Gods (Meter Theon) built in the second half of the 2nd c. B.C., lie in front of the Bouleuterion, on the W side of the Agora. Although the plan of the structure is difficult to distinguish on the ground, it consisted of four rooms with a colonnade on the E side to unify the façade facing on to the square. In the 5th c. the Metroon was converted into a Christian church, to which the mosaic pavement still visible on the site belonged.

Nymphaion

In the 2nd c. A.D. a semicircular fountain-house, the Nymphaion, was built at the SE corner of the Agora, in an area occupied by a number of older buildings: immediately SW a fountain-house (the Enneakrounos?) of the 6th c. B.C., adjoining this a 5th c. structure which was probably a mint (*argyrokopeion*), and to the E a temple dating from the early Roman period. Columns and probably also the cult image from the Doric temple of Demeter and Kore in Thorikos (5th c. B.C.) were used in the construction of this temple; remains of the structure were built into the late Roman "Valerian Wall" (see below).

Above the Nymphaion stands the 11th c. church of Ayii Apóstoli (see entry).

Odeion of Agrippa

A well-preserved Corinthian capital of imposing dimensions marks the position of the Odeion of Agrippa, in the centre of the Agora. Built about 20 B.C. by the Roman general Agrippa, Augustus' son-in-law, it was a rectangular building with a stage and 18 tiers of seating which could accommodate an audience of 1000 (some remains preserved). The entrance was on the S side.

In the 2nd c. A.D. a new entrance was constructed on the N side, with three tritons and three giants supporting the roof of the portico; three of these figures are still erect.

After the destruction of the original building by the Herulians in A.D. 267 the site was used in about 400 for the erection of a Gymnasion to house the University of Athens, which was closed down by the Emperor Justinian in 529; the foundations of this building can still be seen.

Panathenaic Way

According to Pausanias (VIII, 2, 1) the Panathenaic festival in honour of Athena was instituted by Theseus. From the time of

*Panathenaic Way*

*Tholos*

Peisistratos (6th c. B.C.) it was celebrated every four years on the 28th day of the month of Hekatombaion (July–August), Athena's birthday. Starting from the Pompeion in the Kerameikos (see entry), the great Panathenaic procession made its way through the Agora and up to the Acropolis (see entry).

Considerable stretches of the old processional way, with paving of the 2nd c. B.C., are still preserved within the area of the Agora, entering the excavation site at the Altar of the Twelve Gods (see below) and running SE from there.

The remains of this library, built by Flavius Pantaenus in A.D. 100 and destroyed by the Herulians in 267, lie immediately S of the Stoa of Attalos, separated from it by the road leading to the Roman Agora (see entry).

Library of Pantainos

The state prison of Athens has recently been identified by the American archaeologist E. Vanderpool in the new excavation area to the SW of the Agora.

Prison

Going SE from the Tholos for some 100 m (100 yd) alongside the Great Drain, we see on the far side of a bridge (to the left of the drain) a substantial building (37·5 by 16·5 m – 123 by 54 ft) which is dated to the mid 5th c. B.C. This has an open passage down the middle, with spacious cells on either side. The first two rooms on the right of the entrance, which communicate with one another, agree with Plato's description (in the "Crito" and "Phaedo") of the prison in which Socrates spent his last days in the company of his pupils and finally drank the fatal dose of hemlock.

## Agorá

It was long thought that the Royal Stoa (Stoa Basileios) was identical with the Stoa of Zeus (see below), but it has now been located in the new excavation area N of the Piraeus railway. 17·75 m (58 ft) long, it is dated by the excavators to the middle of the 6th c. B.C. It was destroyed in the Persian attack of 470 B.C. but was rebuilt soon afterwards. In the 4th c. B.C. this stoa, like its larger neighbour, the Stoa of Zeus, was extended by the addition of wings on either side.

The Royal Stoa was the seat of the Archon Basileus, who took over the cultic functions of the earlier kings. Among these functions was the trial of offenders accused of *asebeia* (impiety, godlessness); and accordingly this stoa may have been the scene of Socrates' trial in 399 B.C., when he was condemned to death by drinking hemlock, after defending himself against charges of impiety and the corruption of youth in the "Apology" recorded by Plato.

South, Middle and East Stoas

The American excavations have revealed a number of stoas (porticos serving various public purposes) in the southern part of the Agora.

South Stoa I, lying between the earlier Heliaia and fountain-house, was built between 425 and 400 B.C. Situated on the road which bounded the Agora on the S, it was a two-aisled portico with a series of small rooms to the rear.

In the 2nd c. B.C. South Stoa II was built, partly overlapping the site of the first one. This was a single-aisled portico with 30 Doric columns along the open N side.

The Middle Stoa, 146 m (480 ft) long, was built between 175 and 150 B.C. Open on all sides, with Doric columns around the perimeter supporting the roof, this was divided into two aisles by Ionic columns.

The East Stoa, open on the E side, was built about 150 B.C. (after the Middle Stoa but before South Stoa II). Like the other stoas, it was destroyed in 86 B.C. by the Romans under Sulla and thereafter served as a quarry for builders in quest of marble.

Tholos

The most southerly building on the W side of the Agora is the Tholos, a circular structure 18·30 m (60 ft) in diameter. Built around 465 B.C. on the site of an earlier rectangular building, this originally housed the sacred hearth and was the meeting-place of the 50 *prytaneis* (senators) of Athens, a third of whom were required to be in attendance at all times, even during the night; they were accordingly provided with meals and sleeping accommodation in the Tholos.

The roof of the Tholos was supported on six columns. In the 3rd c. B.C. a portico was added on the E side. Rebuilt after its destruction by Sulla in 86 B.C., the building remained in use until about A.D. 450. Only the floor of the Tholos now remains, with an altar in the middle.

Altar of Twelve Gods

The Altar of the Twelve Gods dates from the time of the Peisistratids. In later times it enjoyed the right of asylum, affording sanctuary from pursuit. It was regarded as the central point of Athens, and distances from the city were measured from here.

The remains suffered damage during the construction of the Piraeus railway, and only one corner of the original structure now survives.

The Valerian Wall was a late Roman defensive wall built after the Herulian invasion of A.D. 267, using the remains of destroyed buildings. Fragments can be seen to the S of the Library of Pantainos (see above) and to the E of the Ayii Apóstoli church (see entry).

Valerian Wall

Opposite the Metroon and a few paces E of the Peribolos of the Eponymous Heroes is an altar of Pentelic marble which originally stood on the Pnyx and was later moved to its present site. It is thought to have been dedicated to Zeus as patron of the Agora (Zeus Agoraios).
The oak and laurel trees flanking the altar were planted in 1954 by King Paul and Queen Frederica.

Altar of Zeus Agoraios

The NW part of the Agora, extending to the Piraeus railway line (the construction of which destroyed its N end), is occupied by the Stoa of Zeus Eleutherios (Zeus who maintains the freedom of the city). Originally 46·55 m (153 ft) long, this was built in the 5th c. B.C., in a style reminiscent of Mnesikles' Propylaia on the Acropolis. It had projecting wings at each end, and in front of it, on a round base, stood a statue of Zeus Eleutherios. During the Roman period two rooms were built on to the rear of the stoa, probably for the purposes of the Imperial cult. Pausanias tells us that the Stoa of Zeus contained pictures, including representations of the Twelve Gods, Theseus and the battle of Mantineia.
The earlier belief that the Stoa of Zeus was the same as the Royal Stoa (see above) has been shown by recent excavations to be erroneous.

Stoa of Zeus Eleutherios

## *Agorá Museum                                                    C2

The Agorá Museum is housed in the reconstruction (1953–6) of the Stoa of Attalos (see Agorá), originally built in the 2nd c. B.C. The wealth of material recovered during the Agorá excavations is displayed in the two-aisled stoa and the rooms to the rear.

Stoa
The display of sculpture begins at the S end with the colossal statue of Apollo Patroos (S 2154: 4th c. B.C.), ascribed by Pausanias to the sculptor Euphranor. Then follow a painted Ionic capital (A 2973: 5th c. B.C.); two statues (opposite the second column) representing the Iliad and the Odyssey (S 2038 and 2039: early 2nd c. A.D.); a priestess (opposite the fourth column: S 1016: 4th c. B.C.), flanked by two herms, the one on the right with a hand resting on it which, like Praxiteles' Hermes at Olympia, bears a child (S 33 and 198: Roman); a marble stele inscribed with a law against tyranny and a relief depicting Democracy crowning the people of Athens (by the fifth column: I 6524: 336 B.C.); sculpture from the Temple of Hephaistos (opposite the eleventh column); and acroteria from the Stoa of Zeus (at N end).

**Situation**
In the ancient Agorá

**Electric Railway**
Theseion station

**Opening times**
Mon. and Wed.–Sat. 8 a.m.– 8 p.m.
Sun. 10 a.m.–4.30 p.m.

**Closed**
Tues.

# Agorá Museum

*Stoa of Attalos (Agorá Museum)*

Rear hall
The long main hall to the rear displays in chronological order a large collection of material, most of it notable not so much for its artistic quality as for the evidence it gives on life in ancient Athens.

The collection begins with material of the Neolithic period (3rd millennium B.C.).

The Mycenaean period (1500–1100 B.C.) is represented by vases and grave goods, including two ivory caskets carved with griffins and nautiluses (case 5, BI 511 and 513).

Material of the early Iron Age (11th–8th c. B.C.) includes two 9th c. tombs with their grave goods and Proto-Geometric and Geometric vases (cases 11, 17 and 18). Then come vases in Orientalising style, a mould for casting a bronze statue dating from the Archaic period (6th c. B.C.) and a beautiful 6th c. terracotta figure of a kneeling boy (P 1231).

Here, too, are large numbers of items illustrating the everyday life of the Classical period (5th c. B.C.) – inscriptions, a machine for the selection of public officials by lot (I 3967), sherds used in the process of ostracism (among the names inscribed being that of Themistokles: case 38), etc.

On either side of the exit are cases 61 (finds from a well, ranging in date from the 1st to the 10th c. A.D.) and 63 (material of the Byzantine and Turkish periods).

# Amaroússion (Maroússi)

The suburb of Maroússi occupies the site of the ancient deme of Athmonia, where there was a sanctuary of Artemis Amarysia. In more recent times it has become known through Henry Miller's "Colossus of Maroussi". There are many shops selling local pottery.

**Buses**
19, 121

**Distance**
12 km (7½ miles) N

# * Amphiáreion

The ancient sanctuary of Amphiaraos is beautifully situated in a quiet wooded valley in northern Attica, on the road from the little port of Skála Oropoú to Kálamos and Kapandríti (6 km (4 miles) SE of Skála Oropoú).

**Bus**
To Oropós

**Distance**
45 km (28 miles) N

Amphiaraos was a mythical king of Argos who possessed the gift of clairvoyance. On his way to Boeotia during the expedition of the Seven against Thebes he was victorious in a contest at Nemea during the funeral ceremony of the young prince Opheltes. During the battle for Thebes he was snatched away by Zeus and disappeared into a cleft in the earth. At this spot, on the borders of Attica and Boeotia, where he later re-emerged a sanctuary was established at a sacred spring where he was revered as a seer and as a hero who brought salvation and healing.

**Opening times**
Mon. and Wed.–Sun. 8 a.m.– 1 p.m. and 4–6 p.m.

**Closed**
Tues.

The sanctuary and the cult of Amphiaraos have much in common with the Asklepieion at Epidauros. The site was excavated by Leonardos and Petrakos.

The following are the main features of interest.

A path runs downhill from the entrance to the site, and immediately on the right is the temple (4th or 3rd c. B.C.). This had six Doric columns along the front between antae (pilasters).
The interior is divided into three aisles by two rows of five columns. A porch built on to the rear of the temple contained a second door leading to the priests' quarters. Against the rear wall of the cella can be seen the base for the cult image; in the centre is a table for offerings.

Temple

In front of the temple, beside the sacred spring, is the broad altar, which according to Pausanias was dedicated to Amphiaraos and numerous other divinities.

Altar

Farther along, beyond some statue bases of the Roman period (on left), is the incubation hall in which worshippers seeking a cure slept. The hall, which dates from the 4th c. B.C., is 110 m (360 ft) long and divided into two aisles by a row of 17 Ionic columns, with 41 Doric columns along the exterior. Along the rear wall are stone benches. The two corner rooms were probably intended for women.

Incubation hall

Behind the incubation hall is the theatre, with five marble seats of honour around the orchestra and a well-preserved stage

Theatre

building. The auditorium is overgrown with pines. In this theatre musical contests were held every five years from 332 B.C. onwards.

Baths

Farther down are the remains of Roman baths. On the other side of the little stream are a klepsydra (water-clock) and the remains of houses.

Museum

The small museum contains interesting local finds.

## Anaphiotiká          C2/3

Situation
Pláka

Above the Pláka (see entry), most conveniently reached from the upper end of Erechthéos Street, is this little settlement, established by incomers from the island of Anaphí who came here in the 19th c. and built their little village-style houses on an area of undeveloped land below the Acropolis. Their church of St Simeon, built in 1847, is a plain aisleless structure.

## *Areopagos          C2

Electric Railway
Theseion station

Bus
16

NW of the Acropolis (see entry) is the Areopagos (Areios pagos, Hill of Ares or Mars), seat of the supreme court of ancient Athens. There are three ways of reaching it:

On the S side 16 rock-cut steps (smooth and slippery) lead up to a small plateau surrounded on three sides by further steps leading to the top of the hill.

From the Leofóros Dionysíou Areopagítou, some 150 m (150 yd) to the left (W) of the broad road leading up to the Acropolis, a path runs up in a north-westerly direction through an ancient residential quarter to the foot of the W side of the Areopagos.

Another footpath starts from the Leofóros Apostólou Pávlou, near the SW end of the Agora (see entry) enclosure, and ascends the easy slope of the hillside, past numerous rock cuttings marking the sites of ancient buildings.

The origins of the Areopagos go back to mythical times. Here, according to tradition, Ares was called to account by the gods for the murder of Halirrhotios; and here, too, in Mycenaean times, as Aeschylus relates in his "Eumenides", Orestes stood trial for the murder of his mother Klytaimnestra. The goddess Athena herself secured his acquittal: whereupon the Erinnyes or Furies who had been relentlessly pursuing him – and who had a cave sanctuary on the Areopagos – turned into the Eumenides or "Kindly Ones". The event was commemorated by an altar dedicated to Athena Areia by Orestes, to which Pausanias refers.

A block of stone on the E side of the hill may have been this altar; or alternatively it may have been one of the two stones, the Stone of Wrath and the Stone of Shame, on which the accuser and the accused person sat at trials in historical times. In the 5th c. B.C. the power of the Areopagos was reduced to the role of a constitutional court and a court of morals.

*The Areopagos, seat of the supreme court of ancient Athens*

Chapter 17 of the Acts of the Apostles records the address which the Apostle Paul gave to the "men of Athens" on this ancient sacred site, referring to Christ as the "unknown god" whom they worshipped. A modern bronze tablet (to the right of the steps up the hill) is inscribed with this text.

On the northern slopes of the Areopagos are the remains of a basilica of the Byzantine period dedicated to Dionysios, a member of the Areopagos who – as recorded in the Acts of the Apostles – was one of Paul's first converts (see General, Quotations).

Church of Dionysios the Areopagite

To the SW of the Areopagos, below Leofóros Apostólou Pávlou, an ancient residential quarter has been excavated. On this site, now much overgrown, can be seen a street lined by the remains of substantial buildings (some of them with mosaic floors) and the sanctuary of the old local healing god Amynos, identifiable by its trapezoid plan.
In the northern part of the site is the assembly hall of the Iobakchoi, a Dionysiac fraternity.

Residential quarter

## *Asklepieion                                                        C2

On a narrow terrace above the Stoa of Eumenes (see entry), directly under the steep S face of the Acropolis (see entry), is the Asklepieion, the sanctuary of the healing god Asklepios,

**Situation**
Dionysíou Areopagítou Street

**Bus**
16

**Opening times**
Mon.–Sat. 9 a.m.–6.30 p.m.
Sun. 10 a.m.–4.30 p.m.

whose cult was brought to Athens from Epidauros in 420 B.C. The sanctuary is centred on two sacred springs.

Western part
The earliest part of the sanctuary lay at the western end of the precinct, where there are the foundations of a stoa and a small temple. A number of herms have been brought together in the stoa. At the W end of the complex is a rectangular system with polygonal walls dating from the same period. To the S is a later cistern.

Eastern part
The buildings in the eastern part of the precinct were erected about 350 B.C. Immediately under the Acropolis rock, here hewn into a vertical face, is a stoa 50 m (165 ft) long, originally two-storeyed, designed to accommodate the sick who came here to seek a cure. Associated with it is the cave containing a spring which is still credited with healing powers; and accordingly the cave is now used as a chapel.
Parallel to this stoa, which was rebuilt in Roman times, another stoa was constructed, also in Roman times, on the southern edge of the precinct; of this second stoa some remains survive.

Temple
Both stoas faced towards the centre of the precinct, in which stood the temple. This was oriented to the E and had four columns along the front (prostylos tetrastylos). The foundations of the temple and the altar which stood in front of it are still to be seen. In early Christian times a basilica was built over the remains of the temple and the altar, and some architectural fragments from this can be seen lying about the site.

Bothros
On higher ground at the W end of the stoa is a bothros, a round pit for offerings, originally covered by a canopy borne on four columns. The bothros was an early form of the type of circular structure which reached its finest development in the Tholoi at Delphi and Epidauros.

## Ayía Dýnamis Church          C3

**Situation**
Mitropóleos Street

**Buses**
10, 93/10

This tiny aisleless Church of the Holy Power lies hidden below the modern block occupied by the Ministry of Education. It dates from the Turkish period and has a bell-cote built on to one side.
During the construction of the Ministry building remains of the Themistoclean Walls (see entry) were found. It is thought that one of the 15 gates in the walls, the Diochares Gate, stood near here (junction of Pentélis and Apóllonos Streets).

## *Ayía Ekateríni Church (St Catherine's)          C3

**Situation**
Lysikrátous Street

This church, near Hadrian's Arch (see entry), dates from the 12th or 13th c., with later extensions, and has preserved its original dome and apses.

The church, reached by descending a short flight of steps, stands in a large courtyard planted with palms. In this garden are two columns of the Roman Imperial period; the function of the building to which they belonged is unknown, but it was probably part of an earlier church façade.

**Bus**
16

**Trolleybus**
5

## Ayía Fotiní Church (St Photina's) D3

This little church stands to the E of the Olympieion (see entry) on the busy Leofóros Ardíttou, a modern traffic artery whose construction destroyed the former idyllic charm of the area. The River Ilisos, now canalised, used to flow here, and here, too, was Kallirhoe, the "pleasantly flowing" spring. The spot on the banks of the Ilissos where Socrates liked to talk with his pupils in the shadow of a plane-tree (cf. Plato's "Phaedrus") was either here, according to Rodenwaldt, or farther NE, outside the Stadion, according to Travlos. The church, which is of little architectural interest, is built over the foundations of a temple of Hekate.

**Situation**
Leofóros Ardíttou

**Bus**
12/3

**Trolleybus**
2

## Ayii Anárgyri Church (SS. Cosmas and Damianos) C3

This 17th c. church (with later alterations) in the higher part of the Pláka (see entry) belongs to the monastery of the Panayíou Táfou, a dependency of the Greek Orthodox Monastery of the

**Situation**
Erechtheos Street (Pláka)

*Church of Ayii Apóstoli*

Holy Sepulchre in Jerusalem. It is dedicated to the 3rd c. doctor saints Cosmas and Damian, the "moneyless saints".

The interior is in Baroque style, with a handsome throne and a carved and gilded iconostasis. In the courtyard are some fragments of ancient capitals.

## *Ayii Apóstoli Church                                            C2

**Situation**
In the Agora excavation site

**Electric Railway**
Theseion station

**Buses**
10, 93/10

**Opening times**
Mon. and Wed.–Sat. 9 a.m.–6.30 p.m.
Sun 10 a.m.–4.30 p.m.

**Closed**
Tues.

The Church of the Holy Apostles was the only building left standing when the whole of this quarter of the city was pulled down to permit the excavation of the Agora (see entry). Originally built in the 10th c. over a circular nymphaion (sacred spring) and subsequently much altered, it has been reconstructed in its original form. The exterior is notable for its good ashlar masonry and the ornamental use of Kufic inscriptions.

The dome is borne on four columns, and the apse and transepts have semicircular conches. There are well-preserved frescoes of Christ Pantocrator (Ruler of All: in the dome), John the Baptist, cherubim and archangels. Parts of the original 10th c. iconostasis have been preserved. The paintings in the narthex (17th c.) are from St Spyridon's Church.

## Ayii Asómati Church                                             C2

**Situation**
Ermoú Street

**Electric Railway**
Theseion station

**Buses**
10, 93/10

This little Church of the Incorporeal Beings stands in a little square in the lower part of Ermoú Street, at the junction with Asomáton and Lepeniótou Streets. Like many old buildings in Athens, it now lies below the present street level.

After the Greek war of liberation from the Turks, the church was converted to secular use and was occupied by a pharmacy.

## *Ayii Theódori Church                                           B/C3

**Situation**
Platía Klafthmónos

**Trolleybuses**
1, 2, 5, 12

The Church of SS. Theodore, dedicated to the two military saints of that name, stands at the W end of Klafthmónos Square (see entry), near the University (see entry). Built in the mid 11th c. on the site of an earlier 9th c. church, it is very characteristic of its period: a domed cruciform church with a handsome ashlar exterior, with lines of brick between the courses of stone, a terracotta frieze of animal and plant ornament and Kufic script.

The bell-cote was added later. The interior is modern.

## Ayios Dimítrios Lombardáris Church (St Demetrius)             C2

**Situation**
Apostólou Pávlou Street

**Electric Railway**
Theseion station

**Bus**
16

This little church stands in the gardens on the NE side of the Hill of the Muses (see entry), on the right of the road which runs up to the parking place on the hill. It contains attractive wall paintings.

With its large courtyard, this is one of the churches most frequented by the people of Athens on the occasion of church festivals and processions.

## *Ayios Ioánnistin Kolóna Church (St John of the Column) B2

This little church, standing in a small courtyard, takes its name from the Roman column in the chancel; the column has a Corinthian capital which projects through the roof.
John the Baptist, to whom the church is dedicated, is invoked for all diseases of the head and its organs. Attached to the column with wax are ex-votos in the form of threads, hairs and tablets.

**Situation**
72 Evripídou Street

**Bus**
72

## Ayios Ioánnis Kynigós Church (St John the Huntsman)

The conventual church of St John the Huntsman lies on the northern slopes of Hymettos (see entry), 2 km (1¼ miles) above the village of Ayía Paraskeví, which can be reached from the centre of Athens by way of Vas. Sofías and Messógion Streets. This is a domed cruciform church built in the 12th c. and (as recorded in an inscription) restored in the 13th c., with handsome walls of dressed stone. The limewashed narthex was added in the 17th c. The 17th c. frescoes in the interior area, unfortunately, partly covered with whitewash.

**Bus**
44, Marathon

**Distance**
10 km (6 miles) NE of city centre

## Ayios Ioánnis o Theológos Church (St John the Evangelist) C3

This beautiful 13th c. domed cruciform church, with Roman capitals, stands in a little square at the intersection of Erechthéos and Erotokrítou Streets, in which a mulberry tree provides welcome shade. The church was restored some years ago.

**Situation**
Erechthéos Street (Pláka)

## *Ayios Nikodímos/Sotíra tou Lykodímou (St Nicodemus) C3

This domed cruciform church is one of Athens' numerous 11th c. churches. Erected in 1045 (the date is recorded in an inscription), it was damaged by the Turks in 1780, purchased by the Tsar of Russia in 1845 and redecorated internally by the painter Ludwig Thiersch. Since then, re-dedicated to St Nicodemus, it has belonged to the Russian Orthodox Church. Immediately adjoining the church are ancient remains which, according to Travlos, belonged to baths attached to the Lykeion (Lyceum).

**Situation**
Filellínon Street

**Buses**
16, 165

**Trolleybuses**
2, 5, 12

## Ayios Nikólaos Rangavá Church (St Nicholas) C3

Between the churches of Ayios Ioánnis o Theológos (see entry) and Ayios Yeóryios tou Vráchou (see entry) stands this 11th c. church. It was attached to the palace of the Rangava family, which produced several Byzantine Emperors and Oecumenical Patriarchs.
Much altered in later centuries, the church is now being restored.

**Situation**
Prytaníou Street (Pláka)

# Ayios Yeóryios Vráchou (St George of the Rock)  C3

**Situation**
Epichármou Street (Pláka)

This tiny aisleless church, probably dating from the Frankish period, stands at the top of the stepped Epichármou Street, on the upper edge of the Pláka (see entry). It takes its name from its situation immediately below the rock-face of the Acropolis. There is another church dedicated to St George on Lykabettos (see entry).

# *Benáki Museum  C4

**Situation**
Leofóros Vas. Sofías

**Buses**
3A/7A

**Trolleybus**
3

**Opening times**
Daily 8.30 a.m.–2 p.m.

**Closed**
Tues.

The Benáki Museum, based on the private collection assembled by Antonios Benáki, displays on three floors a varied range of exhibits – relics of the Greek war of independence, mementoes of kings Otto and George I, Byron and others who fought for independence, manuscripts and icons (including two attributed to the young El Greco), costumes from various parts of Greece, ancient pottery and Islamic and East Asian material.

Ground floor
Room $A$: War of Independence
Room $B$: Liturgical objects brought to Greece by refugees from Asia Minor (including an epitaphios from Constantinople, 17th c.: case 25)
Room $\Gamma$: Icons by Michael Damaskinos
Room $\Delta$: Coptic cloths, Coptic and Islamic ivories, mummy portraits
Room $E$: Reception hall from a Cairo house, Rhodian pottery
Room $AA$: Hellenistic, Roman, early Christian and Coptic material, mementoes of Venizelos
Room $BB$: Ancient pottery and bronzes

Upper floor
Room $Z$: Icons
Rooms $H–\Theta$: Objects which belonged to King Otto and Queen Amalia, Byron, etc.
Room $I$: Mementoes of George I and the Cretan risings
Room $K$: Two early icons by El Greco
Room $\Lambda$: Islamic and Persian cloths
Room $M$: Hellenistic and Byzantine textiles
Room $N$: Mycenaean, Byzantine and Islamic jewellery, a Helladic gold cup
Room $\Xi$: Chinese pottery and porcelain
Room $O$: Handicrafts of the Greek islands
Room $\Pi$: Egyptian and Persian pottery, 18th and 19th c. pictures

Basement
Costumes and ornaments from all parts of Greece, two 18th c. reception rooms from Kozáni

There is a cafeteria on the flat roof of the Museum.

## * **Brauron** (modern Greek Vrávron or Vráona)

Brauron, on the E coast of Attica 5·5 km (3½ miles) NE of Markópoulo, was of importance in ancient times for its sanctuary of Artemis. Excavated by Papadimitriou between 1948 and 1963 and excellently restored, it is now a most impressive and interesting site.

**Bus**
To Vrávron

**Distance**
33 km (20 miles) E

**Opening times**
Mon.–Sat. 8 a.m. to sunset
Sun. 10 a.m.–1 p.m. and
3–6 p.m.

The site of Brauron was occupied from Neolithic times. Remains of Middle Helladic buildings (2000–1600 B.C.) were found on the acropolis, and there was evidence of dense settlement in the Late Helladic (Mycenaean) period (1600–1100 B.C.). After a period of abandonment the site was resettled in the 9th c. B.C. Brauron's heyday was in the 5th and 4th c., but after 300 B.C. the land became waterlogged and was again abandoned. The cult of Artemis Brauronia was taken from Brauron to the Acropolis of Athens in the 6th c. by Peisistratos, a native of Brauron.

In Mycenaean times the goddess Artemis was known here as Artemis Iphigeneia; and according to Euripides Iphigeneia, daughter of king Agamemnon of Mycenae, was a priestess at Brauron after her return from the Tauric Chersonesos until her death. During the Classical period Athenian girls aged between 5 and 10 served in the sanctuary. They were known as "little bears" (arktoi) from the saffron-coloured garments they wore, recalling a she-bear sacred to Artemis.

At the foot of a hill near a 12th c. chapel of St George (restored) is a small shrine, behind which are the Cave of Iphigeneia (now roofless) and a "sacred house".

Cave of Iphigeneia and Sacred House

To the N are the rock-cut footings of the temple of Artemis, built in the first half of the 5th c. B.C. on the site of an earlier structure.

Lower down is a courtyard surrounded on three sides by colonnades, built between 430 and 420 B.C. The entrance is on the W side, where there is an ancient stone bridge. The Doric columns of the colonnades, of limestone, had marble capitals. Six rooms in the N wing and three in the W wing each contained eleven wooden beds for the "little bears".

Courtyard

The Museum contains finds from the site:
Rooms 1–3: Material from the sanctuary of Artemis.
Room 5: Pottery found on the acropolis, of Early to Late Helladic date (3rd millennium to 1100 B.C.); pottery from Anávyssos and the Peráti necropolis.
Atrium and Room 4: Material from the Merénda necropolis (vases of the 9th–4th c. B.C.).

Museum

500 m (540 yd) inland are the excavated remains of an early Byzantine church (6th c.), a three-aisled basilica with a narthex and exonarthex. The E end, separated from the rest of the church by a screen, is closed by an apse, in which the semicircular seating for the officiating clergy (synthronon) can still be seen. At the E end of the S aisle is a small chapel, also with an apse. At the E end of this aisle is a doorway leading into the circular baptistery.

Early Byzantine church

The basilica was evidently destroyed after a relatively short period of existence. Thereafter a small chapel, of which some remains survive, was built in the centre of the nave.

*Icons from the Byzantine Museum*

# *Byzantine Museum                                           C4

**Situation**
Leofóros Vas. Sofías

**Buses**
3A/7A

**Trolleybus**
3

**Opening times**
Weekdays 8 a.m.–3.30 p.m.

**Closed**
Sundays and holidays

This valuable collection of Byzantine art from Greece and Asia Minor is housed in a palace built by Kleanthes in 1840, on a site which was then in open country, for the eccentric Duchesse de Plaisance, wife of Charles-François Lebrun, whom Napoleon made Duc de Plaisance (Piacenza).

Courtyard: Architectural fragments from Early Christian basilicas and Byzantine churches (5th–15th c.) and a reproduction of a fountain depicted in a mosaic at the monastery of Dafní (see entry).

The left-hand wing contains a large collection of icons.
Room 1: A range of icons on the Life, Passion and Resurrection of Christ; the Trinity; Christ Pantocrator (Ruler of All); Life of the Mother of God; various saints.
Room 2: Icons of the 16th and 17th c., including St Anthony (T 211), the Panayía Kardiótissa (T 1582), St John the Evangelist (T 1052) and St Eleutherius (T 144).
At one end of the room are an iconostasis and (to the right of this) a small tripartite altar (400).
On the right-hand wall are the Life of the Mother of God (T 1561) and the Hospitality of Abraham (T 590).
Room 3: Icons by Constantine and Emmanuel Tsanes.
Room 4: Icons of the 17th and 18th c.

The right-hand wing contains late Byzantine and post-Byzantine icons (13th–16th c.).
There is a particularly interesting group opposite the entrance: a 12th c. icon of the Mother of God, with the version overpainted in the 17th c., which has recently been detached.

Main building (ground floor): The rooms on this floor illustrate the development of the church interior.
Room 1: A scaled-down reconstruction of an early Christian basilica, with the templon, the screen which separates the chancel (bema), in which are the altar and the seats for the clergy (synthronon), from the rest of the church.
Room 3: A typical Middle Byzantine domed cruciform church (10th–11th c.), with a sculptured eagle on the floor marking the omphalos (navel).
Room 4: Example of a post-Byzantine church (17th–18th c.) with a carved and gilded iconostasis.
Individual items of particular interest:
Room 1: Sculptured representations of the Good Shepherd (92), in which the old type of the lamb-carrier (see Acropolis Museum) is applied to Christ, and Orpheus (93).
Room 2: Byzantine reliefs, including a number of rare relief icons.

Main building (upper floor): Numerous icons.
Room 1: A mosaic icon of the Mother of God Episkepsis (145: 14th c.), Gospel books, historical documents (among them a chrysobull of the Emperor Andronikos II dated 1301).
Room 2: Gold jewellery from Lesbos.
Room 4: Liturgical utensils and vestments (particularly notable being a 14th c. epitaphios from Salonica – an embroidered pall used in the representation of the Holy Sepulchre on Good Friday); wall paintings from Oropós.

## Cemetery of Athens (Próton Nekrotafíon Athinón)     D3/4

Immediately S of the Olympieion (see entry) Anapáfseos Street (the "Street of Repose") branches off Ardíttou Street, a busy traffic artery, and runs up to the principal Athenian cemetery. After passing through the modern entrance hall we see on the left, near a chapel, the tombs of the archbishops of Athens. Then follows the imposing monument of George Averoff, who financed the construction of the modern Stadion and other buildings. On the slope beyond this is the Temple-like tomb of Heinrich Schliemann, designed by Ernst Ziller. Nearby is the tomb of Admiral Kanáris. On the left of the central avenue running down to the second chapel is the tomb of Kolokotrónis, one of the great heroes of the War of Independence.

**Situation**
Anapáfseos Street

## Constitution Square

See Sýntagma Square.

## **Dafní

**Buses**
68, 100

**Distance**
10 km (6 miles) W

**Opening times**
now closed

The monastery of Dafní, 10 km (6 miles) W of the city centre, is famous for its 11th c. mosaics. The name recalls that this was the site of a sanctuary of Apollo, to whom the laurel (*daphne*) was sacred. The pagan shrine gave place to an early Christian monastery, which in 1080 was replaced by the present monastery, dedicated to the Dormition of the Mother of God (*koimesis, kímisis*), the Orthodox equivalent of the Assumption of the Virgin. In 1205, after the Frankish occupation of Athens, it was handed over to Cistercians from Burgundy and became the burial place of the Frankish lords (later dukes) of Athens. From this period date the battlemented defensive walls and a number of sarcophagi. At the beginning of the Turkish period the monastery was reoccupied by Orthodox monks. During the 19th c. war of liberation Dafní suffered damage and was abandoned. A thorough restoration in 1955–7 saved the buildings from further dilapidation. Both the church and the precinct wall were damaged by an earthquake in 1981.

Courtyard

The picturesque and attractive courtyard of the monastery is bounded on the W by one side of the cloister, on the N by the S wall of the church and on the E by other monastic buildings. From the W entrance we pass through the Gothic exonarthex, dating from the period of Cistercian occupation, and the narthex into the church, which ranks with Osios Loukás near Delphi and the Néa Moní on Chios as one of the three finest 11th c. Byzantine churches.

Naos

The naos, on a Greek cross plan, is dominated by the large central dome which spans both the central aisle and the two lateral aisles. From the dome the grave and majestic figure of

# Dafní
## Church

### ICONOGRAPHY

1 Last Supper, Washing of the Feet, Betrayal
2 Presentation of the Virgin, Blessing of the Priests, Joachim and Anna
3 Elpidophorus, Pegasius, Bacchus, Aphthonius
4 Dormition
5 Orestes, Mardarius, Sergius, Auxentius
6 Andronicus, Tarachus, Probus; Crucifixion, Raising of Lazarus, Entry into Jerusalem
7 Pantocrator and Prophets
8 Annunciation
9 Nativity
10 Baptism of Christ
11 Transfiguration

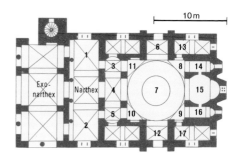

12 Samonas, Guriel, Abibus; Descent into Hell, Incredulity of Thomas, Christ in the Temple
13 Nativity of the Virgin
14 John the Baptist, Silvester, Aaron, Stephen, Zacharias, Anthimus

15 Mary, Michael, Preparation of the Throne, Resurrection, Gabriel
16 Nicholas, Eleutherius, Gregory the Wonderworker, Lawrence, Avercius, Gregory of Agrigento
17 Magi

*Dafní: the Gothic exonarthex (porch)*

Christ Pantocrator looks down. In the pendentives under the dome are four of the major themes of Orthodox iconography – the Annunciation (NE), Nativity (SE), Baptism of Christ (SW) and Transfiguration (NW).

Of the numerous other mosaics the following are particularly notable:

Other mosaics

N arm of cross: Raising of Lazarus, Entry into Jerusalem (NW), Nativity of the Virgin and Crucifixion (NE).
S arm of cross: The Magi, the Risen Christ (SE), the Presentation in the Temple and the Doubting of Thomas (SW).
Chancel: Mary between the Archangels Michael and Gabriel.
Prothesis and diakonikon: Saints.
Above door of naos: Dormition.
Narthex: Prayer of Joachim and Anne, Presentation of Virgin.
All these scenes show 11th c. mosaic art at its peak, in a fascinating blend of the Greek sense of beauty and Christian spiritualisation.

From July to September the adjoining Tourist Pavilion is the scene of a Wine Festival, with free wine-tasting, Greek culinary specialties, music and dancing.

## Daou Pendéli Monastery

See Pentélikon

# Dexameni Square (Platía Dexamenís)    C4

Bus
50

Dexameni Square, situated above Kolonáki Square at the foot of Lykabettos (see entry), is named after an ancient reservoir associated with an aqueduct constructed by the Emperor Hadrian (2nd c.). The aqueduct was brought back into use in the 19th c. The reservoir – now a small public garden – was embellished with an Ionic propylon, destroyed in the 15th c., of which a few remains survive.

# Dionysios the Areopagite, Cathedral of (St Denis)    C3

Situation
Panepistimíou (Venizélou)
Street
Bus
16
Trolleybuses
1, 2, 3, 5, 12

Like the basilica on the northern slopes of the Areopagos (see entry), this Roman Catholic cathedral is dedicated to Dionysios the Areopagite (St Denis). It is a three-aisled basilica without transepts, fronted by a Corinthian arcade. Built in 1853–87, it was designed by Leo von Klenze.

# Dionysius

Distance
22 km (14 miles) N

Situated at an altitude of 460 m (1510 ft) on the N side of Pentélikon (see entry), on the road from Drosiá to Néa Mákri, is the village of Dionysius, one of the most popular places of resort around Athens. On the outskirts of the village is a sanctuary of Dionysos, which belonged to the ancient city of Ikaria, home of Thespis, who produced the first tragedy in Athens in 534 B.C. The introduction of vine-growing was attributed to king Ikarios.

# *Eleusis (Elefsís)

Railway
Athens–Corinth

Bus
68

Distance
22 km (14 miles) W

Opening times
Mon.–Sat. 9 a.m.–3 p.m.
Sun. 10 a.m.–4.30 p.m.

Ancient Eleusis has given its name both to the modern town of Elefsís and to the bay on which it lies. But this whole stretch of coast is so disfigured by refineries and other industrial installations that visitors arriving here will find it difficult to believe that they are approaching the site of an important ancient sanctuary.

Excavation has revealed the sanctuary, frequented from Mycenaean times onwards, which was the home of the famous Eleusinian mysteries. The Eleusinian cult arose out of the myth of the goddess Demeter, who lamented at the Kallichoron well here the loss of her daughter Persephone, abducted by Hades; and no corn grew on the earth until Zeus commanded that Persephone should be allowed to return above ground annually in spring. Demeter thereupon established the Eleusinian mysteries, in which she was honoured as the granter of fertility and Persephone (also known as Kore, the Maiden) as an annually returning vegetation goddess. The intiates of the mysteries, who were admitted in two stages to the Lesser and the Greater Eleusinia, appear to have been given the promise not only of the annual renewal of nature but also of a

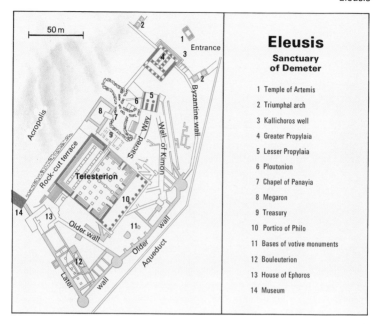

**Eleusis**
**Sanctuary of Demeter**

1 Temple of Artemis
2 Triumphal arch
3 Kallichoros well
4 Greater Propylaia
5 Lesser Propylaia
6 Ploutonion
7 Chapel of Panayia
8 Megaron
9 Treasury
10 Portico of Philo
11 Bases of votive monuments
12 Bouleuterion
13 House of Ephoros
14 Museum

resurrection. But the study of the mysteries has been hampered by the strict secrecy observed by the initiates and maintained into late antiquity.

From the entrance to the site we come first to remains dating from the Roman period – two triumphal arches and between them the Greater Propylaia, a gateway in the old precinct wall of the sanctuary built in the reign of Antoninus Pius (A.D. 138–161) in imitation of the Propylaia on the Acropolis of Athens. The pediment was set to the right of the entrance, which was approached by a broad flight of steps. In the interior of the marble Propylaia are five gateways.

*Greater Propylaia*

To the S of the Propylaia (outside the precinct wall) and on a lower level can be seen the circular mouth of the Kallichoron well at which Demeter lamented the loss of her daughter. In order to avoid disturbing this ancient structure the base of the Propylaia was cut away. Behind the well is the polygonal wall built by Kimon in the 5th c. B.C.

*Kallichoron well*

Beyond the Greater Propylaia we come to the Lesser Propylaia (54 B.C.). To the right, on the slopes of the hill on which the ancient city lay, is the Cave of Pluto, the legendary entrance to the underworld. On the hill is a chapel of the Panayía (Mother of God), occupying the site of a Roman megaron. From here the Sacred Way leads to the central feature of the sanctuary, the Telesterion.

*Lesser Propylaia*

*View of the Bay of Eleusis from outside the Museum*

Telesterion

In this hall, concealed from the eye of the non-initiate, the mysteries were celebrated. The Solonic Telesterion was erected about 600 B.C. on the site of a small Mycenaean temple of the 14th c. B.C., with an Anaktoron (holy of holies) which remained until Roman times the central element in the structure. Remains of these earlier buildings were found near the E corner of the Telesterion.

Various additions and alterations were carried out in the 6th and 5th c. Peisistratos enlarged the Telesterion into a square structure measuring 27 m (89 ft) each way, with five rows of five columns supporting the roof. After suffering damage during the Persian wars the building was enlarged again by Kimon, to become a rectangular structure 27 by 44 m (89 by 144 ft), with three rows of seven columns. Finally Pericles restored the square plan, with the dimensions that can be seen today (54 by 52 m – 177 by 171 ft) and seven rows of six columns (traces of which can be seen on the ground). Between 330 and 310 B.C. the Portico of Philo was added on the SE side.

Round the hall ran tiers of seating, those hewn from the rocky hillside being still preserved. Recent Greek excavations have identified the position of the Anaktoron.

Museum

A rock-cut flight of steps leads up to the Museum, in the forecourt of which are statues and a sarcophagus with a representation of the hunting of the Calydonian boar.

Entrance hall: figure of Demeter attributed to Phidias' pupil Agorakritos (*c.* 420 B.C.); cast of votive relief of Demeter, Persephone and the boy Triptolemos (440 B.C.: original in National Archaeological Museum – see entry).

Room I (to right): Sculpture from the pediment of Peisistratos' Telesterion; statue of Persephone (480 B.C.); archaic kouros from Megara (530 B.C.). In the centre of the room is a Proto-Attic amphora from Eleusis (650 B.C.), with Odysseus blinding Polyphemos (above) and Perseus killing the Medusa (below).

Room II (to left): Archaic kore; statue of Asklepios (c. 320 B.C.); statue of an ephebe by Lysippos (?); Roman statuette of Dionysos.

Room III: Statues of the Roman period; two reconstructions of the sanctuary.

Room IV: Caryatid from the Lesser Propylaia (54 B.C.); terracotta sarcophagus containing the remains of a child; bronze vase containing human remains; marble slab with a miniature-scale bust and pithos (storage jar); Corinthian amphora (7th c. B.C.).

Room V: Pottery from Eleusis, dating from Mycenaean times onwards.

## Gennadiós Library

B/C5

This library, assembled by a former Greek ambassador in London, Gennadiós, and donated by him to the American School of Classical Studies in 1923, is housed in a neo-classical building erected by the Carnegie Foundation. It is a specialised library on Greece, with more than 50,000 volumes in many different languages.

**Situation**
Gennadioú Street

**Bus**
50

*Gennadiós Library*

*Hadrian's Arch*

## Hadrian's Arch                                                           C3

**Situation**
Leofóros Amalías

**Buses**
16, 84, 63/64

**Trolleybuses**
2, 5, 12

To the W of the Olympieion (see entry), immediately adjoining the Leofóros Amalías, one of Athens' busiest traffic arteries, is Hadrian's Arch, erected in A.D. 131–132, when the gigantic temple of Olympian Zeus was finally completed. It is thought to occupy the position of an earlier city gate of the 6th c. B.C., and was later incorporated by the Turks in the circuit of walls with which they surrounded the town in 1778 and which was pierced by seven gates.

The arch is a plain structure of Pentelic marble, bearing two inscriptions: on the W side, facing the Acropolis, "This is the ancient city of Theseus", and on the E side, facing the Olympieion, "This is the city of Hadrian and not of Theseus".

## Hill of the Muses (Mouseion) and Philopappos Monument   C/D2

**Bus**
16

The Hlll of the Muses is part of a chain of low hills to the SW of the Acropolis, the others being the Pnyx and the Hill of the Nymphs (see entries). From the top of the hill (147 m – 482 ft) there is the classic and beautiful view of the Acropolis, with Lykabettos rearing up behind (see entries).

From Dionysíou Areopagítou Street, at the point where it joins Apostólou Pávlou Street, a road branches off and goes up to a parking place on the far side of the hill. From here a path runs E along the rocky hill to the prominent monument of Philo-pappos, a prince of Commagene (SE Anatolia) who was banished to Athens by the Romans and died there in A.D. 116. In gratitude for his munificence the Athenians allowed his ostentatious tomb to be erected on this exceptional site – an honour, it has been remarked, that was not granted even to a man like Pericles in the great days of Athens. On the frieze around the base Philopappos is shown in the guise of a Roman consul, mounted in a chariot and accompanied by lictors. Above this are seated figures of the dead man and (to the left) Antiochos IV, his grandfather.

On the way to (or from) this monument of the personality cult under the Roman Empire, there can be seen some remains of the *diateichisma*, the intermediate wall built in 337 B.C. to shorten the defensive lines between the Long Walls. Here too are various cisterns and rock-cut chambers, one of them traditionally misnamed the Prison of Socrates (now identified to the SW of the Agora – see entry).

## Hill of the Nymphs (Lófos Nimfón)     C2

At the western end of the chain of hills which runs SW of the Acropolis is the Hill of the Nymphs, easily identifiable by the domed Observatory on the summit. It is reached by way of a side street off Apostólou Pávlou Street.

**Bus**
16

The classical-style Observatory was built by Theophil Hansen in 1843–6 to the design of Schaubert. To the right of the entrance are the remains of the ancient sanctuary of the Nymphs from which the hill takes its name – a levelled rock surface and a dedicatory inscription. This level platform on the highest point of the hill was chosen by Ferdinand Stademann in 1835 as the viewpoint from which to draw his "Panorama of Athens" (republished 1977).

To the SE the Hill of the Nymphs merges into the Pnyx (see entry). From both hills there are fine views of Athens.

## Hymettos (Imittós)

The plain of Athens is bounded on the E by the long ridge of Hymettos (1027 m – 3370 ft), made up of the bluish-grey Hymettian marble, overlying Pentelic marble, which was worked in ancient times. The hills were then covered with forest, and the honey of the region was renowned.

In recent decades efforts have been made to replant trees on the deforested slopes of the hill, particularly around Kaisarianí monastery (see entry). The monastery has an abundant spring, one of the many once found on Hymettos.

On the summit plateau there was a sanctuary of Zeus Ombrios, who was invoked with prayers for rain. Other shrines on Hymettos were the precinct of Apollo Proopsios and, at the southern end of the range, the Cave of the Nymphs (3 km (2 miles) N of Vári).

There is now a road which leads from the suburb of Kaisarianí, on the E side of Athens, to Kaisarianí monastery and continues

to Astéri monastery (16th c. church, with frescoes), ending on the summit plateau (military area, closed to the public).
Below the N side of the hill is another monastery, Ayios Ioánnis Kynigós (see entry). It can be reached from the village of Ayía Paraskeví on the road from Athens to Markópoulo (2 km (1¼ miles) before Stavrós).

## *Kaisariani Monastery

**Bus**
39 (to suburb of Kaisariani, then 30 minutes' walk)

**Distance**
7 km (4 miles) E

**Opening times**
Mon.–Sat. 8.30 a.m.–12.30 p.m. and 4–6 p.m.
Sun. 9 a.m.–3 p.m.

Kaisariani monastery lies beyond the eastern suburb of Kaisariani, which is named after it, and is reached on a road which runs past this monastery and the monastery of Astéri (16th c. domed cruciform church, with frescoes), higher up, to the summit plateau of Hymettos (see entry; 1027 m (3370 ft): military area, closed to public).
The name comes from a spring close to a sanctuary of Aphrodite from which the emperor Hadrian caused an aqueduct to be built to supply Athens: thereafter the spring was known as *kaisariane*, Imperial. It was (and is) credited with healing powers, particularly for women who desire to bear a child. The water still flows from an ancient ram's head in the courtyard of the monastery.

Church

The monastery church is of the domed cruciform type. It was erected about the year 1000 on the site of an earlier church, and is thus rather older than the buildings of this type in Athens itself. The dome is borne not on the walls but on four columns with Ionic capitals, giving the interior an air of lightness. A templon formed of marble screens separates the chancel (bema) from the rest of the church.
The painting is much later than the church itself, having been done in the 16th c., during the Turkish period, probably by a monk from Athos. It is in strict accordance with the rules for the hierarchical disposition of the various subjects – Christ Pantocrator in the dome, with the Prophets round the windows and the four Evangelists in the pendentives; the Mother of God enthroned in the apse, with angels, the Communion of the Apostles and the fathers of the church below her; and on the barrel-vaulting of the arms of the cross the various church festivals. The figures stand out vividly against a black ground. In the porch is a fine representation of the Trinity. The porch, like the S chapel dedicated to St Antony and the bell-cote, was added in the late 17th c.

Conventual buildings

There are well-preserved remains of the conventual buildings. Entering by the main entrance, on the E side, we see on the left a building which was originally a bath-house (on the Roman plan, with hot, cold and warm baths) and later housed oil-presses. Beyond this, set back a little, are a two-storeyed range of cells and a tower house belonging to the Venizelos family of Athens, who were great benefactors of the monastery. In the right-hand corner are the kitchen and refectory (now a museum).

On the hill outside the W gateway of the monastery (15 minutes' walk) are other remains of churches dating back to the 6th c., beside the monks' cemetery. From here there are extensive views of Athens.

## Kanellópoulos Museum                                      C3

The important private collection assembled by Paul and
Alexandra Kanellópoulos and now belonging to the state is
housed in a neo-classical mansion on the upper edge of the
Pláka, near the Metamórfosis church (see entries). It is of
interest for its displays of both ancient and Christian art.

Basement: Icons, including the very beautiful wonder-working
icon of the Panayía Myrtidiotissa (1747), a rare iconographic
type.

Ground floor: Icons, liturgical utensils, silver and gold
jewellery, embroidery; Egyptian mummy portraits and a
painted death mask, a head of the Emperor Galerius (4th c. A.D.)
and Byzantine coins (pre-1204).

First floor: Antiquities, including Greek pottery from the
Geometric period onwards; pottery and metalwork from
Cyprus; small marble Cycladic idols and stone implements and
utensils of the Cycladic culture (3rd c. B.C.); Egyptian items in
wood and metal.

Second floor: Pottery from Cyprus, Asia Minor, Corinth and
Crete; Attic pottery (e.g. a vase with Priam, Hector and
Andromache), a head of Alexander and Tanagra figurines.

**Situation**
Corner of Pánou and Theorías
Streets
(Pláka)

**Opening times**
Weekdays 8.30 a.m.–
12.30 p.m. and 4–6 p.m.
Sun. 9 a.m.–3 p.m.

---

## Kapnikaréa Church                                         C3

In a little square, opening off Ermoú Street, stands this
interesting church, now the University church, which was
saved from destruction during the construction of Ermoú Street
in the 19th c. only by the intervention of King Ludwig I of
Bavaria.
The Kapnikaréa is a very fine example of a domed cruciform
church of the 11th c., with the little chapel of St Barbara on the
N side. In the 12th c. a narthex with four pediments (originally
open) was built on to the W end, giving architectural unity to
the church and chapel. The graceful entrance portico appears
to date from the same period.
The paintings in the interior (19th c.) cover the complete
iconographic programme as developed in the Middle Byzantine period.

**Situation**
Ermoú Street

**Bus**
10

---

## *Kerameikos Cemetery                                      B/C2

Kerameikos, the potters' quarter of ancient Athens, was named
after Keramos, the patron of potters, and has, appropriately
given its name to the art and craft of ceramics. It was bounded
on the NW by the Agora and extended westward as far as the
Academy (see entries). After 479 B.C., when, following the
Persian invasion, Themistocles enclosed the city within walls,
part of the area lay within the walls and part outside them.

**Situation**
Ermoú Street

**Electric Railway**
Theseíon station

**Buses**
10, 72

# Kerameikos Cemetery

**Opening times**
Tues.–Sat. 9 a.m.–3 p.m.
Sun. 10 a.m.–4 p.m.

**Closed**
Mon.

From the 12th c. onwards this area, on both banks of the Eridanos brook, was used for burial, and a continuous sequence of tombs can be traced from sub-Mycenaean times to late antiquity. The monumental funerary amphoras ("Dipylon vases") of the 8th c. B.C., which can be regarded as the starting point of Attic funerary art, are now in the National Archaeological Museum (see entry), and the remains visible on the site are predominantly of the 5th and 4th c. B.C. The tombs are of many different types – individual tombs, funerary precincts, terraces of tombs – represented either by the originals or by copies.

This is the most thoroughly excavated of the cemeteries of Athens, by Greek archaeologists from 1863, by German archaeologists from 1907. Only part of the old Kerameikos quarter has been excavated – the area lying in the angle between Ermoú and Pireós Streets, beside the Ayía Triáda church. The residential area beyond the town walls, between the Sacred Gate and Ermoú Street, is at present under excavation. The whole site, still little affected by mass tourism, is quiet and full of atmosphere, although the surrounding area is not particularly attractive.

Dipylon

There are two gates through the walls at this point, the Dipylon and the Sacred Gate. The walls themselves were built by Themistocles in 479 B.C. and were strengthened in the 4th c. B.C. by the construction of outworks and moats.

The more northerly of the two gates, and the one of greater architectural consequence, is the Dipylon, the largest of the city gates of ancient Athens. As its name indicates, it is double, with a rectangular court between the two gates. Inside the inner gate are an altar dedicated to Zeus, Hermes and Akamas (son of Theseus) and a fountain-house.

Street of Tombs

The cemetery area is traversed by three roads – the road to the Academy, to the N; the Sacred Way, farther S, which ran from the Dipylon to Eleusis (see entry); and the Street of Tombs, which branched westward off the Sacred Way in the direction of Piraeus. All three of these roads are lined with tombs.

Going N from the entrance (past the Museum) on an ancient road, we pass on the left the tomb of two sisters, Demetria and Pamphile (c. 350 B.C.), and come to the Street of Tombs, with burials of the 5th and 4th c. B.C. (mostly 4th c.). Turning W (left) along this road, we pass on the left the equestrian monument of Dexileos (original in museum: see below), the tomb of Agathon and Sosikrates of Herakleia in Pontos (with three stelae) and the tomb of Dionysios of Kollytos, topped by a bull. Beyond this is the burial plot of Archon Lysimachides of Acharnai, built of polygonal blocks, guarded by a Molossian hound and decorated with reliefs (Charon, a funeral meal), and beyond this again is a crudely constructed altar belonging to a cult precinct of Hekate.

Returning along the same road, we see on the left two interesting family burial plots – the first belonging to the family of Eubios (stele of Bion) and the other to the family of Koroibos; this has a funerary stele in the middle, a relief of Hegeso (cast: c. 410 B.C.) on the left and a loutrophoros (a large water jar for the bridal bath, set over the tomb of a person who died unmarried) on the right. Then follows (just before a side street on the left) a large round tumulus of the 6th c. B.C. belonging to one of the great families of the period. To the E,

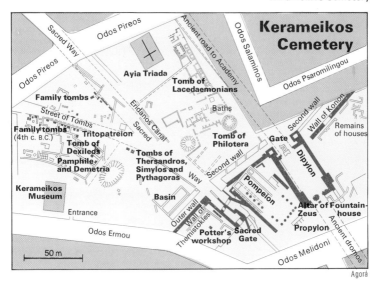

Agorá

beyond the Eridanos, are the remains of another circular tomb, perhaps a heroon. Also on the left of the road is the small trapezoid sanctuary of the Tritopatores (ancestor gods), with inscribed boundary stones at the NE and SE corners. Beyond this, on the right, are the simple tombs of envoys from Kerkyra (*c*. 375 B.C.) and of Pythagoras of Selymbria (*c*. 450 B.C.) and a walled triangular cult precinct of unknown dedication. On the hillside behind this is an aqueduct. The Street of Tombs now runs into the Sacred Way.

The Sacred Way, which leaves Athens by way of the Sacred Gate, is so called because it was the route followed by the solemn procession from the city to the sanctuary of the mysteries at Eleusis (see entry). To the NW are the tombs of Antidosis and Aristomache and beyond these the handsome loutrophoros of Olympichos. In the other direction, towards the city, the Sacred Way runs alongside the Eridanos to the Sacred Gate.

Sacred Way

The Sacred Gate, through which the processions to Eleusis left the city, is in the SE part of the excavation site. There are two gateways. One of these spans the Eridanos on vaulting which is still preserved, and to the right of this is the main carriageway.

Sacred Gate

The Museum, at the entrance to the site, contains the more recent finds; older finds are in the National Archaeological Museum (see entry). The museum is notable for the large collection of pottery, illustrating both the history pf the Kerameikos area and the development of Greek pottery types.

Museum

The first room contains sculpture from tombs. Above the entrance doorway is a fragment from the Tomb of the

Lacedaemonians (with the names of two fallen polemarchs in a script running from right to left). Immediately to the right of the entrance is the stele of Ampharete, showing the dead woman with her infant grandchild (*c.* 410 B.C.), and opposite this are a bronze cauldron (5th c. B.C.), an equestrian relief of Dexileos, killed in a skirmish at Corinth in 394 B.C., and the stele of Eupheros (430 B.C.). Here, too, are a series of items of the Archaic period, including a seated figure with remains of colouring (530 B.C.) on the left-hand wall; a poros stele (570–560 B.C.) and a statue base carved with an equestrian procession (550 B.C.) in the centre of the room; and on the window side of the room another base with a wild boar fighting a lion (520–510 B.C.) and a sphinx (550 B.C.), the original colouring of which is shown in a reconstruction drawing on the wall. On the rear wall is the figure of a horseman (520 B.C.), and in the passage leading to the pottery collection is the head of a contestant in the pentathlon (560–550 B.C.).

Outside the museum, to the N, is a collection of modest funerary colonnettes (*kioniskoi*) – simple monuments set up after a sumptuary law of 317 B.C. banning the lavish tombs which had reflected 400 years of development of Athenian funerary art.

To the left of the entrance to the Museum is a low hill which affords an excellent view of the whole site.

**Pompeion**

Between the walls, the Sacred Gate and the Dipylon is the Gymnasion on the Eridanos, usually known as the Pompeion – the starting point of the procession (*pompe*) which made its way during the Panathenaic festival (Agora (see entry), Panathenaic Way) from here across the Agora to the Acropolis. There are remains of two buildings, one overlying the other. The earlier one, dating from about 400 B.C., consisted of a court surrounded by colonnades (6×13 columns): i.e., it was a gymnasion. Objects used in the Panathenaic procession were kept here. Wheel-ruts in the propylon show that the court was entered by wheeled vehicles. The rooms on the N side were probably the scene of the ceremonial banquet at the end of the festival; and it has been suggested (by Hoepfner) that the Panathenaic vases which were the prizes for victors in the contests may have been presented here.

This earlier building was destroyed by Sulla in 86 B.C., and much later, in the 2nd c. A.D., replaced by a three-aisled hall, which in turn was destroyed by the Herulians in A.D. 267.

The ground plans of the two overlapping buildings can be understood most clearly from outside the site, in Melidóni Street (turn left along Ermoú Street when leaving the site and then immediately left again).

**Road to the Academy**

On either side of the Dipylon two *horos* (boundary) stones set against the town walls mark the breadth (39 m – 128 ft) of the road which runs from here to the Academy (see entry). Along this road men who had fallen in war were buried in common graves, which were regarded with special honour. It was on one such occasion, at the beginning of the Peloponnesian War (431 B.C.), that Pericles gave the famous funeral oration which

*Kerameikos: burial plot of the family of Koroibos* ▶

is recorded by Thucydides. None of these graves of special honour has yet been found, but excavation has brought to light, at the second boundary stone on the S side of the road, the state tomb of the Lacedaemonians – the Spartan officers who died in 403 B.C. in the fight against the Thirty Tyrants of Athens.

Just on the edge of the excavated area are the remains of another (anonymous) tomb. Pausanias refers to other tombs of special honour on the road to the Academy, including that of Harmodios and Aristogeiton, murderers of the tyrant Hipparchos.

# Kifissiá

**Electric Railway**
Kifissiá station

**Buses**
18A, 49

**Distance**
14 km (9 miles) N

The villa suburb of Kifissiá, situated at an altitude of 276 m (880 ft), is popular with both Athenians and visitors on account of its pleasant climate. In 1979 the remains of a large Roman bath-house of the 2nd c. A.D. were found here – probably belonging to a summer villa described by Aulus Gellius, the property of Herodes Atticus, a portrait bust of whom was found here in 1961 together with a bust of his pupil Polydeukes. In the square, under a protective roof, are a number of sarcophagi decorated with garlands which date from the same (Roman) period.

# King Otto Museum                                          B/C3

**Situation**
Klafthmónos Square

**Trolleybuses**
1, 2, 5, 12

**Opening times**
Mon., Wed. and Fri. 9 a.m.–
1.30 p.m.

The King Otto Museum was opened in December 1980 as the first part of a new Museum of Athens. It occupies the modest mansion, built in 1834, in which King Otto and Queen Amalia resided from 1836 until 1842, when they moved into the newly built palace in Sýntagma Square. The last descendant of the original builder (Stamatios Vouros), Lambros Evtaxias, had it restored to its original form by the architect Jannis Travlos, using the plans of its original German architects, Lüders and Hoffer, and made it available to house the museum.

On the ground floor visitors can see the old kitchen. On the first floor are the apartments used by the royal couple, with their Empire and Biedermeier furniture – the Queen's room, the drawing-room, the King's study, the audience chamber, the room of the gentleman-in-waiting, the dining-room. In addition to numerous mementoes and pictures of King Otto's time (1815–67, reigned 1833–67), including loans from the Bavarian State Collections, the museum contains an interesting model of Athens in 1842, on a scale of 1:1000.

# Klafthmónos Square (Platía Klafthmónos)            B/C3

**Trolleybuses**
1, 2, 5, 12

The SW side of this square, with the church of Ayii Theódori (see entry), borders the older part of the town (see Pláka). Along with the National Library, the University and the Academy, with which it is linked by Korai Street, it forms part of the replanned Athens of the first part of the 19th c.

In ancient times the boundary of the city ran through this area, and a section of the Themistoclean town walls of 479 B.C. can be seen in the square and at 6–8 Dragatsaníou Street (on the NW side of the square).

King Otto and Queen Amalia lived from 1836 to 1842 in a modest mansion (see King Otto Museum) at the S corner of the square, next the only surviving classical-style building.

The first Greek Ministry of Finance also stood in the square, and its name (*klafthmon*, "lamentation") refers to the complaints by government officials over the non-payment of their salaries. Beneath the centre of the square is a large underground car park.

## Kolonáki Square                                            C4

This square, situated in the embassy quarter between Leofóros Vas. Sofías and Lykabettos, was for long a favoured residential district. In the gardens in the centre stands the small column from which it takes its name, and all round are the cafés and restaurants which make the square a popular place of resort for both young people and their seniors.

**Bus**
50

## *Library of Hadrian                                       C3

Parallel to the Roman Agora (see entry), only 16 m (50 ft) away, is another complex of similar character but different function – the Library of Hadrian, founded by the emperor of that name after A.D. 132. This was a colonnaded court measuring 122 by 82 m (400 by 270 ft), with exedrae (semicircular recesses) in the external walls. The entrance was on the W side, and part of this, richly decorated with Corinthian columns and a four-column propylon, has been preserved. It faces on to Areos Street, which runs S from Monastiráki Square past the old Sindrivani Mosque (now housing the Museum of Ceramics). New excavations are in progress here.

The modern entrance to the site (at present closed) is at the E end, in Eólou Street.

The central room in the E range of buildings, much of which is still standing, was the actual library, and the niches in which the book rolls were kept can still be recognised. The building as a whole was not designed, like the Roman Agora, for business purposes, and the spacious courtyard was laid out as a garden, with a pool in the middle. The columns and other architectural fragments now to be seen in the courtyard came from the Megáli Panayía church, which was built in the 5th c. on the site of the original pool.

**Situation**
Eólou Street

**Buses**
10, 72

**Opening times**
At present closed

## Loútsa

Behind the dunes at the coastal resort of Loútsa, 9 km (5½ miles) E of Spáta and the same distance N of Brauron (see entry), a Doric temple of the 4th c. B.C. was discovered in 1956.

**Bus**
96

*Lykabettos: St George's Chapel*

**Distance**
30 km (19 miles) E

It was probably dedicated to Artemis Tauropolos, for whom, according to Euripides, Orestes built a temple after returning from Tauris with his sister Iphigeneia and landing at Brauron. Loútsa is the ancient Halai Araphenides, where it is known from inscriptions that a festival of Dionysos was celebrated as well as the festival of Artemis, the Tauropolia.

## Lykabettos (Likavittós)                                         B4/5

**Trolleybus**
50

Lykabettos (277 m – 909 ft), once well outside Athens but now surrounded by the city on all sides, is the dominant hill in the plain of Attica. The road to the hill, which is signposted from Leofóros Vas. Sofías, leads to the end of Ploutárchou Street, from which a cable railway ascends in a tunnel to the summit. There is also a footpath from Dexameni Square (see entry). Refreshments are available on the top of the hill. From the whitewashed chapel of St George there are extensive views over Athens, which is especially impressive at night.

## *Lysikrates, Monument of                                        C3

**Situation**
Lysikrátous and Tripódon
Streets

The Monument of Lysikrates stands in a little square at the end of Lysikrátous Street. This rotunda, 6·50 m (21 ft) in height and 2·80 m (9 ft) in diameter is surrounded by what appear to be pilasters but are in fact fully rounded Corinthian columns, between which curved marble slabs have been inserted. Round the top runs a frieze depicting scenes from the life of Dionysos (the transformation into dolphins of the pirates who had captured the god). The stone acanthus flower on the roof originally bore a bronze tripod, the prize received by Lysikrates when the choir which he had financed as *choregos* was victorious in the tragedy competition in 334 B.C.

In 1669 the monument was acquired by a Capuchin convent and used as a library, when it became known as the "Lantern of Diogenes".

This is the only surviving example of the numerous choregic monuments in the ancient Street of the Tripods (which was on roughly the same line as the present street of that name). Other choregic monuments in Athens are the Monument of Nikias beside the Stoa of Eumenes (see entry) and the Monument of Thrasyllos above the Theatre of Dionysos (see entry).

Immediately above the gardens in the little square is one of the few Karagiósis theatres still in operation. These shadow plays with their stock characters, represented by figures of coloured leather, are derived from the Turkish Karagöz ("Black-Eye").

**Buses**
31/58

**Trolleybuses**
1, 2, 5, 12

## *Marathon

Marathon ("field of fennel") lies on the E coast of Attica, in an area in which a whole series of holiday resorts have developed in recent years, extending from Schiniás by way of Paralía Marathónos (Marathon Beach) and Néa Makrí to Ayios Andréas and Máti.

Marathon was famed in ancient times as the place where Theseus killed the bull of Marathon and as the scene of the first great battle between Greeks and Persians in September 490 B.C. In this battle the Athenians, supported by a contingent from Plataiai, defeated the numerically much superior army of the Persian Empire. Ten years later the Persians launched a further attack, but were again defeated at Salamis (480) and Plataiai (479).

In later antiquity Marathon was the home of Herodes Atticus (A.D. 101–177), noted as a rhetor but still more famous for his munificence (see Odeion of Herodes Atticus; see Stadion).

Apart from the present-day village, the name of Marathon is associated with two ancient sites, the Soros (burial mound) of the Athenians and the Soros of the Plataeans at Vranás, and with the modern reservoir (Lake Marathon). The village lies 5 km (3 miles) from the coast on the road which runs N to Grammatikó.

**Bus**
To Marathon

**Distance**
41 km (25 miles) NE

**Opening times**
Museum: Mon. and Wed.–
Sat. 8.30 a.m.–12.30 p.m.
and 4–6 p.m.
Sun. 10 a.m.–4.30 p.m.

**Closed**
Tues.

The battlefield of 490 B.C. is 5 km (3 miles) S of the village, between the Athens–Marathon road and the coast. The site is marked by the 12 m (40 ft) high burial mound of the 192 Athenians who fell in the battle. Greek excavations in 1890 brought to light the remains of the dead, together with sacrificial animals and pottery. At the foot of the mound is a copy of the funerary stele of Aristion, carved *c.* 510 B.C. (original in National Archaeological Museum, Athens).

From the top of the mound there are extensive views of the surrounding area – to the NE the wide bay with the beach at

Battlefield

Schiniás where the Persians landed and pitched camp; to the W the Vranás area, at the foot of Agrielíki and Pentélikon, where the Greeks were positioned at the start of the battle. The burial mound itself marks the spot where the decisive encounter took place.

**Burial mound of the Plataeans**

3 km (2 miles) N of the Athenian burial mound the "Plataean Road" (Leofóros Plateion) turns W off the road to the village of Marathón and in 2·5 km (1½ miles) reaches the little hamlet of Vranás. To the left (signposted), surrounded by trees, is the burial mound (excavated 1970) of the Plataeans who fell in the battle. It has a diameter of 40 m (130 ft) and stands 4 m (13 ft) high. A dromos leads into the mound (now closed), in which the remains of eleven of the twenty or so Plataeans who fell have been left. In the interior, which is electrically lighted, can be seen the tomb of an officer named Archias (on right) and that of a 14-year-old boy, whose remains are partly covered by a large pottery vessel.

**Museum**

At the end of the hamlet of Vranás can be seen a large barn-like structure erected over the site of a cemetery of the Middle and Late Helladic periods (2000–1100 B.C.). Adjoining it is the Marathon Museum, opened in 1975, which has a fine collection of local finds, arranged in chronological order in five rooms (going in an anti-clockwise direction).

Entrance hall: Map of the area; copies of a Persian helmet and of the "Ephebe of Marathon" (original in National Archaeological Museum, Athens).

Rooms *A* and *B*: Neolithic and Early Helladic pottery (4000–2000 B.C.), mainly from the Cave of Pan and the Tsepi necropolis; Middle and Late Helladic material (2000–1100 B.C.) from Vranás; Geometric pottery from Marathon.

Room *Γ*: Finds from the Athenian and Plataean burial mounds; terracotta figurines from the Cave of Pan (6th–5th c. B.C.).

Room *Δ*: Funerary relief of a young man with a child and a dog (*c.* 350 B.C.) and other funerary reliefs.

Room *E*: Over-lifesize male figure in Egyptian-influenced style (2nd c. A.D.); female statue (Isis?); child's tomb; portrait busts; glass.

On the hillside W of Vranás is the little nunnery of Ayios Yeóryios.

**Lake Marathon**

The reservoir known as Lake Marathon lies 8 km (5 miles) W of the village of that name on the road to Ayios Stéfanos. It was formed by the construction in 1926–31 of a dam 285 m (310 yd) long and 72 m (235 ft) high. Set amid extensive pine forests, it is the main source of Athens' water supply. (Bathing and boating prohibited.)

---

## Metamórfosis Church (Church of the Transfiguration)                    C2

**Situation**
Theorías and Klepsidras
Streets (Pláka)

This little domed cruciform church stands at the upper end of Klepsídras Street, which runs up from the Tower of the Winds (see entry) to a point immediately below the rock-face of the Acropolis. It can also be reached by taking the panoramic road (Theorías Street) which begins between the Propylaia (see Acropolis) and the Areopagos (see entry).

Although built in the 14th c., during the period of Frankish rule, the church is purely Greek in character. An early Christian capital serves as the altar of this modest place of worship.

## Military Museum                                              C4/5

The Military Museum, opened in 1975, is housed in a modern building between the Byzantine Museum (see entry) and the Hilton Hotel. The collection illustrates the story of the wars in which the Greeks have been involved, some of them of decisive importance for Greece itself (e.g. Navarino, 1827), others of major significance in world history (e.g. the Persian wars of the 5th c. B.C.), and emphasising the continuity of Greek history down the centuries.

The visit begins on the main floor, in the long Hall A, on one side of which is a cast of the frieze of the Temple of Apollo at Bassai (original in the British Museum). Here, too, are stone and bronze weapons of Neolithic and Mycenaean times, Corinthian helmets (5th c. B.C.) and material relating to the battles of Marathon, Thermopylai and Salamis (490–480 B.C.). The other rooms continue in chronological order through the period of Alexander the Great, the Byzantine era, the periods of Frankish and Turkish rule, the War of Greek Independence and the fight for independence in Crete and Macedonia to the Second World War and Greek participation in the Korean war.

**Situation**
Leofóros Vas. Sofías

**Trolleybuses**
3, 7

**Opening times**
Tues.–Sat. 9 a.m.–2 p.m.
Sun. 9.30 a.m.–2 p.m.

**Closed**
Mon.

## *Mitrópolis                                                   C3

In Mitrópolis Square, which is reached from Sýntagma Square by way of Mitropóleos Street, are two churches of very different character – the medieval Little Mitrópolis and the modern Great Mitrópolis.

**Situation**
Platía Mitropóleos

**Electric Railway**
Monastiráki station

### Little Mitrópolis

The 12th c. Little Mitrópolis, a tiny domed cruciform church only 11 m (36 ft) long by 7 m (23 ft) wide, is dedicated to the Panayía Gorgoepikoós (the Mother of God as the Swift Hearer of Prayer) and St Eleutherius, both of whom offer help to women in childbirth. This Christian church thus continues an ancient tradition, since the sanctuary of the Greek goddess Eileithyia, likewise the patroness of childbirth, was also located here. It is known as the Mitrópolis because it belonged to the monastery of St Nicholas, the residence of the metropolitans (archbishops) of Athens in the 18th and early 19th c. The monastery was destroyed in 1827, during the war of independence, and its site is now occupied by the Great Mitrópolis.

The church is unique in that it is not built of the usual dressed stone and brick but of fragments taken from ancient and medieval buildings. Above the entrance can be seen two parts of an ancient calendar frieze (arranged in the wrong order) with

91

*Great and Little Mitrópolis*

*Little Mitrópolis*

relief representations of the months, flanked by two pilaster capitals. Elsewhere are a variety of figural reliefs, including a figure of Cybele enthroned (in pediment on E side), fragments of funerary aediculae, etc. Many of the ancient fragments have been "Christianised" by having crosses carved on them.

Compared with the fascination and charm of the exterior, the interior of the church, restored in recent years, is of little interest.

## Great Mitrópolis

The Great Mitrópolis occupies the site of the monastery of St Nicholas which was destroyed in 1827. It is dedicated to the Annunciation (Evangelismós), which is represented above the main doorway, but is also known as St Nicholas in memory of the former monastery.

The church was built between 1840 and 1855 to the design of Schaubert, who set out to give the new capital of Greece a cathedral worthy of its status. The exterior displays the eclecticism of the 19th c., the interior its leaning towards a rather sombre magnificence. Beside the first pillar on the left is the tomb of Patriarch Gregory IV, who in 1821 was hanged by the Turks in Constantinople and is honoured as a neomartyr. (There is a statue of him in front of the University – see entry.) The principal festivals of the Greek Orthodox Church are celebrated in the Great Mitrópolis in the presence of the head of state.

## Monastiráki Square                                    C2

In this square, named after the monastery to which the Pantánassa church (see entry) belonged, all the different phases of the history of Athens are represented. In the middle of the square is the Pantánassa, a foundation dating back to the 10th c. At the SE corner is one of the city's two surviving mosques, known as the Sindrivani after the former purification fountain, and which now houses the Ceramic collection of the Museum of Popular Art. Immediately behind the mosque, in Areos Street, is the pillared façade of the Library of Hadrian (see entry), a monument of the Roman period; and farther S is Athens of the Classical period, with the Acropolis (see entry). Finally there is the Electric Railway station to represent the modern age.

The square itself and the adjoining streets and lanes are a centre of busy commercial activity.

To the N is Athinás Street, a busy thoroughfare which runs N to Omónia Square (see entry) through the bazaar-like market area.

To the E is Pandrósou Street, with its numerous small shops selling icons and small antiques as well as souvenirs and jewellery.

In the little streets to the W the flea-market has been established; here one can buy every conceivable variety of second- and third-hand object. Here, too, in Adrianoú Street, are the shops specialising in copper ware.

**Electric Railway**
Monastiráki station

**Buses**
10, 72

---

## Moní ton Klistón (Convent of the Gorges)

Going NW from the village of Filí (or Chassiá) in the direction of ancient Phyle (see entry), we come in 4 km (2½ miles) to Moní ton Klistón, the Convent of the Gorges (on right). After passing a large modern school building we reach this small well-preserved nunnery, perched on the rim of the deep gorge of the River Gouras. The 14th c. domed cruciform church is dedicated to the Dormition of the Mother of God (Kímisis tis Theotókou).

From the courtyard there is a cableway over the gorge to a spot marked with a white cross on the vertical rock-face opposite, where, according to tradition, an icon was found which led to the establishment of the nunnery. The cableway is used to take burning candles across to this inaccessible spot.

Higher up the gorge was a cave sacred to the shepherd god Pan, the setting of Menander's comedy "Dyskolos".

**Bus**
To village of Filí

**Distance**
18 km (11 miles) NW (to Filí); then 4 km (2½ miles) to convent

---

## **National Archaeological Museum                    B3

The National Archaeological Museum, built by Ludwig Lange in 1860 and since then considerably enlarged, contains the largest collection of Greek art in the world. Repeated visits are necessary to get anything approaching a complete idea of the wealth of its collections. Here it is possible to do no more than draw attention to a selection of the most notable exhibits.

**Situation**
Leofóros Patissión

**Trolleybuses**
2, 3, 12

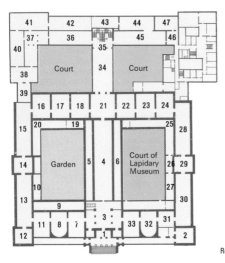

# National Archaeological Museum

1 Entrance
2 Shop
3 Entrance hall
4 Mycenaean art
5 Neolithic art
6 Cycladic art
7–13 Archaic art
14, 15 First half of 5th c.
16–20 Classical period (5th c.)
21 Diadumenos and other statues
22 Sculpture from Epidauros
23, 24 Funerary stelae (4th c.)
25–27 Votive reliefs (4th c.)
28 Ephebe of Antikythira
29 Themis (3rd c.)
30 Hellenistic art
32 Stathatos Collection
34 Votive reliefs
35 Stairs to upper floor
36 Karapanos Collection
37 Small bronzes
45 Bronze statues

Rooms not listed are not at present open to the public

**Opening times**
Weekdays 9 a.m.–4.30 p.m.,
Sun. 10 a.m.–2 p.m.

**Closed**
Tues.

Room 4, the *Mycenaean Hall*: Material excavated by Schliemann and others at Mycenae and other Mycenaean sites, illustrating the richness of the Mycenaean culture, which combined the nobility and monumentality of Achaean Greek art with the refinement of Minoan Crete (1600–1150 B.C.). The exhibits are not arranged chronologically but according to sites or types of material. The front part of the hall is occupied by material from Mycenae itself, including the famous gold mask of a king from Shaft Grave V (252: *c.* 1580 B.C.), together with gold cups, vases, carved ivories, richly decorated daggers, boar's-tusk helmets, the "Warrior Vase" (1426: *c.* 1200) and two pilasters from the entrance to the "Treasury of Atreus". Particularly notable items in the rear part of the hall are the two famous gold cups (1758, 1759) from Vaphìò, S of Sparta, which date from the 15th c. B.C.

Room 5 (to left), the *Neolithic Hall*: Material from the Greek mainland including objects from Dimini (4th millennium B.C.), Sesklo (3rd millennium B.C.) and Orchomenós (3rd–2nd millennium B.C.).

Room 6 (to right), the *Cycladic Hall*: Material of the 3rd and 2nd millennia B.C. from the Cyclades. Characteristic of the highly developed art of this insular culture are the "Cycladic idols" and "Cycladic pans", ritual objects associated with the cult of the dead and of the gods. Notable items are the Harp-Player (3908) and the flying-fish frescoes from Phylakopi on the island of Milos (5844: 16th c. B.C.).

Returning to the entrance hall, we continue clockwise through the chronologically arranged collections, beginning with the Geometric period (9th–8th c. B.C.) and continuing through the Archaic (7th–6th c.) and Classical (5th–4th c.) to the Hellenistic (3rd–1st c.) and Roman periods.

Room 7: In the centre is the Dipylon Vase from the Kerameikos cemetery, a monumental sepulchral vase in Geometric style with a representation of the lament for the dead, dating from the time of Homer (V 804: *c.* 750 B.C.).
On the right-hand wall is a flat, almost board-like, relief from the island of Delos, dedicated by Nikandre (1: *c.* 650 B.C.).
Metopes from the Archaic temple of Athena at Mycenae (2702, 2869, 2870, 4471: *c.* 620 B.C.).

Room 8 is dominated by two kouroi from Soúnion, some 3 m (10 ft) high (2720, 3645: 625–600 B.C.). When Greek artists began to produce large sculpture after 650 B.C. they achieved monumental expression in over-lifesize figures of naked youths (kouroi). Characteristic of these figures are the rigidly frontal pose and the equal distribution of weight on both legs, with the left foot always in front of the right. Originally the hands were held close to the thighs, with clenched fists; later the arms hung free.
Also in this room are the head and hand of a kouros from Kerameikos (the "Dipylon Head", 3372: *c.* 600 B.C.).

Room 9 (to right): Winged Nike (Victory) from Delos (21: *c.* 500 B.C.) and, to right, a slender kouros from Milos (1558: *c.* 550 B.C.).
Of particular interest is the excellently preserved kore holding a lotus flower in her left hand, with an inscription giving her name as Phrasikleia (4889). This figure was found by Mastrokostas in 1972 at Merénda, near Markópoulo in Attica.

Room 10: The kouros in this room (4890) was also found at Merénda. Stylistic comparisons suggest that the figure of Phrasikleia was carved about 530 B.C. by Aristion, a sculptor from Paros working in Attica who was also responsible for the figure of Kroisos from Anávyssos in Room 13. In Andrew Stewart's view the Merénda kouros and the Theseus and Antiope group from Eretria (Chalkis Museum) are also by Aristion or his school.
Also in this room is a fine ephebe with a discus from the Dipylon (*c.* 560 B.C.).

Room 11: Stele of Aristion, by Aristokles (29: *c.* 510 B.C.); kouros from the island of Kea (3686: *c.* 530 B.C.).

Room 12: Relief of a running hoplite from Athens (1959: *c.* 510 B.C.); heads from the E pediment of the Temple of Aphaia, Aegina.

Room 13: More kouroi, including a late Archaic figure with arms akimbo from the Ptoion (127: *c.* 510 B.C.) and a powerful figure from Anávyssos by Aristion of Paros (3851: *c.* 540 B.C.), with an inscription on the base: "Stop at his grave and weep for the dead Kroisos, destroyed by wrathful Ares while fighting among the warriors in the forefront of the battle."

Room 14: Classical art, including a relief of Aphrodite (?) from Milos (3990: 470–460 B.C.) and a relief of a youth with a garland (originally a metal attachment) from Soúnion (3344: *c.* 470 B.C.).

Room 15: Eleusinian votive relief (on left) depicting Demeter giving the first ear of corn to the boy Triptolemos, with her daughter Persephone or Kore (126: *c.* 440 B.C.).
In the centre of the room is an imposing over-lifesize bronze statue of a god (15161) found in the sea off Cape Artemision (northern Euboea); it was previously identified as Zeus but is now generally recognised as representing Poseidon. The latest research indicates that it was made after the battle of Plataiai (479 B.C.) as an offering to the sanctuary of Poseidon on the Isthmus or to a sanctuary on Cape Artemision.

Room 16: Funerary monuments, including a large marble lekythos from the tomb of Myrrhine (4485: *c.* 420 B.C.).

Room 17: Votive relief from Piraeus depicting Dionysos with actors (1500: *c.* 400 B.C.); head of Hera from the Argive Heraion (1571: *c.* 420 B.C.).

Rooms 19 and 20 (to side): Votive relief with figures of Demeter and Persephone (3572: 420 B.C.); torso of Apollo of the "Kassel Apollo" type (1612: Roman copy of a Greek original of the 5th c. B.C.); votive relief dedicated to Pan and the nymphs, from the S face of the Acropolis (1329: 410 B.C.); the "Varvakion statuette", a small Roman copy of Phidias' Athena Parthenos (129: 2nd–3rd c. A.D.).
From here we can enter one of the inner courts of the Museum.

*Fresco from Akrotiri on Santorin (upper floor) and Ephebe of Antikythera (Room 28)*

Room 18: Relief of Hegeso and her maid, the most famous of the Kerameikos monuments (3624: c. 410 B.C.).

Room 21: The Diadumenos, a Roman marble copy of a lost bronze original by Polykleitos (1826: c. 440 B.C.), and (straight ahead) the Hermes of Andros, a Roman copy of an original of the school of Praxiteles (218: 4th c. B.C.) – two works which exemplify the change from the vigorous but controlled physical representations of the 5th c. to the spiritualised approach of the 4th. Also in this room is the boy rider (15177: 2nd c. B.C.), recently mounted on a horse which is well restored but is not his original mount.

Room 34: Votive reliefs dedicated to Pan and the nymphs.

Rooms 36 and 37: The Karapanos Collection, with numerous small bronzes of the Archaic and Classical periods, including a horseman from Dodona (16547: c. 550 B.C.), a goddess with a dove (Aphrodite or Dione) from the Pindos (460 B.C.) and the famous statuette of Zeus hurling a thunderbolt from Dodona (16546: 450 B.C.).
Other notable items in this room are an Archaic head of Zeus from Olympia (6440: c. 550 B.C.) and a number of pieces of sculpture from the Acropolis, including a male head with inlaid eyes (6446: c. 490 B.C.), the head of a youth (6590: 480 B.C.), also with inlaid eyes, and an Athena Promachos (6447: c. 450 B.C.).

Room 40: Large bronzes, including an Apollo (c. 510 B.C.), two figures of Artemis (4th c. B.C.), found by chance in Piraeus in 1959, and the Ephebe of Marathon, probably by Praxiteles or his school, which was recovered from the sea in 1925 (c. 350 B.C.).

We now return to the main circuit.

Room 22: Sculpture from Epidauros.

Rooms 23 and 24: Funerary stelae of the 4th c. B.C., including the Ilissos Stele, perhaps by Skopas (578: c. 350 B.C.).

Room 25 (to side): Statuettes and other votive objects dedicated to Amynos and Asklepios.

Room 28: The Ephebe of Antikythera, an original work in bronze, probably representing Paris or Perseus and carved by Euphranor (Br 13396: 340 B.C.).
At the end of the room are a figure of Hygieia, probably by Skopas (3602: c. 360 B.C.) and a head of Asklepios from the island of Amorgos (4th c. B.C.).

Room 29: A large group from the sanctuary of Despina at Lykosoura (Peloponnese) and a large statue of Themis from Rhamnous (231: early 3rd c. B.C.).

Room 30: Poseidon of Milos (235: 2nd c. B.C.); bronze heads of a boxer from Olympia (Br 6439: c. 350 B.C.), a philosopher (Br 13400: 3rd c. B.C.) and a man from Delos (Br 14612: c. 100 B.C.).

Room 32: Helene Stathatos Collection, with items ranging in date from prehistoric to Byzantine times.

On the upper· floor (reached from Room 34) are three collections of particular interest:
the Museum's very comprehensive collection of vases;
the sensational finds which have been made since 1967 at Akrotiri on the island of Santorin; and
material from the Cyprus National Museum in Nikosia.

Special collections

Other special collections housed in the Museum are:
the Epigraphical Collection (open daily in summer 7.30 a.m.–3 p.m., closed Sun.; in winter daily 8 a.m.–2 p.m., closed Sun.);
the Numismatic Museum (open daily in summer 7.30 a.m.–3 p.m., winter 8 a.m.–2 p.m., closed Sun.); and
the Cypriot Coin Collection (open daily in summer 7.30 a.m.–3 p.m., winter 8 a.m.–2 p.m., closed Sun.).

---

# National Gallery C4

**Situation**
Leofóros Vas. Konstantínou

**Trolleybuses**
3, 7

**Opening times**
Tues.–Sat. 8.30 a.m.–
12.30 p.m.
Sun. 4 a.m.–8 p.m.

**Closed**
Mon.

The National Gallery (Alexandros Soutsos Museum) is housed in a new building in Leofóros Vasiléos Konstantínou.

On the ground floor are icons and pictures by Greek painters of the 19th and 20th c. (historical and genre pictures, seascapes, portraits).

On the upper floor are pictures by European painters, including Caravaggio, Tiepolo, Rembrandt, Breughel and Jordaens, and among the moderns Picasso, Braque and others. Works by the Cretan-born El Greco occupy a place of honour.
There are also works by many Greek painters, including Nikólaos Gízis, Nikifóros Lýstras, Andréas Kriézis, Vikéntios Lántsas and Simeon Savvídis. Visitors are likely to be particularly interested in their pictures on Greek subjects (scenes from the everyday life of the people, the ever popular theme of the Acropolis).

In the basement are a collection of graphic art and special exhibitions, as well as a cafeteria.

---

# National Garden (Ethnikós Kípos) and Záppion C3/4

**Situation**
Main entrance in Leofóros
Amalías

**Buses**
16, 84

**Trolleybuses**
2, 5, 12

The National Garden was originally laid out by Queen Amalia, wife·of King Otto, and together with the adjoining Záppion garden it was the only large open space in Athens until the area extending from the Agora to the Hill of the Muses (see entries) was laid out as a park in quite recent years.
To the S of the National Garden are the gardens around the Záppion, an exhibition hall with a Corinthian portico and a semicircular colonnade to the rear built by Ernst Ziller for the Zappas brothers.

*The Záppion exhibition hall in the National Garden*

## National Historical Museum

Old Parliament

## New Palace (Néa Anáktora) C4

The New Palace, on the E side of the National Garden (see entry), was built in 1890–8 by Ernst Ziller (who also designed Schliemann's house (see entry) and other buildings in Athens) as the Crown Prince's Palace. It became the royal palace in 1935 after the restoration of the monarchy, and since 1974, when Greece became a Republic, it has been the official residence of the President. In front of the palace Evzones in their traditional costumes mount guard.

**Situation**
Iródou tou Attikoú Street

**Buses**
12/3

## *Odeion of Herodes Atticus C2

The large complex of buildings on the S side of the Acropolis extends from the Theatre of Dionysios at the E end by way of the Stoa of Eumenes (see entries) to the youngest of the three structures, the Odeion of Herodes Atticus, at the W end. This is

**Situation**
Dionysíou Areopagítou Street

**Bus**
16

99

named after the wealthy and munificent Herodes Atticus of Marathon (101–177), who built it after the death of his wife Regilla in 161.

Its proximity to the Theatre of Dionysos (see entry) provides a convenient demonstration of the difference between the Greek and Roman methods of theatre construction.

**The Greek theatre**

The Greek theatre fitted its auditorium into a natural hollow, and the rows of seating extended round more than a semicircle. The orchestra was originally exactly circular, as at Epidauros, and the low stage structure (*skene*) lay close to it on one side, only loosely connected with it. Between the auditorium and the stage were open passages for the entrance of the choir (*parodoi*).

**The Roman theatre**

The principles of Roman theatre construction, as exemplified in the Odeion of Herodes Atticus, were quite different. The auditorium (*cavea*) was exactly semicircular, the side entrances were vaulted over and the stage, which in the later period was increased in height, was backed by an elaborate stage wall (*scenae frons*) of several tiers, lavishly decked with columns and statues, which rose to the same height as the top rows of seats or the enclosure wall of the auditorium. The auditorium and the stage thus formed an architectural unity, and the theatre became a totally enclosed space. The theatre was open to the sky, but an odeion (odeon), intended for musical performances, would be roofed.

The 32 steeply raked rows of seating in the Odeion of Herodes Atticus (recently restored with a facing of white marble) could accommodate an audience of 5000. The structure, which was incorporated in the defences of the medieval castle, is in such an excellent state of preservation that it is used during the Athens Festival every summer for dramatic performances and concerts by leading Greek and European artistes.

---

## *Old Palace (Paleá Anáktora)                                          C3/4

**Situation**
Sýntagma Square

**Bus**
16

**Trolleybuses**
1, 2, 5, 12

After consideration had been given to siting the royal palace of the new kingdom of Greece in Omónia Square and at the W end of Ermoú Street, it was finally built (by Friedrich von Gärtner, 1836–42) on the E side of Sýntagma Square (see entry), the driest site in Athens. Laid out around two courtyards, it is 115 m (377 ft) long by 95 m (312 ft) deep. It lacks the decorative features originally designed for it by Leo von Klenze, apart from the 21 m (70 ft) long portico of ten Doric columns fronting the square and the 44 m (144 ft) long S gallery, with sixteen Doric columns, which faces the National Garden.

The palace was occupied by Otto and George I, but in 1935 the royal family moved into the Crown Prince's Palace (see New Palace) and the Old Palace became the seat of the Greek Parliament, which still meets here.

To the S and E of the Old Palace extends the National Garden (see entry), originally laid out by Queen Amalia on what was then waste ground.

*Odeion of Herodes Atticus: a theatre of Roman type* ▶

*The Old Parliament, now housing the National Historical Museum*

## Old Parliament (Voulí) and National Historical Museum     C3

**Situation**
Plateia Konokotrónis, Odnos Stadíou

**Trolleybuses**
2, 5, 12

**Opening times**
Temporarily closed for repairs

The Old Parliament (Voulí), which now houses the very fine collections of the National Historical Museum, was built in 1858–74 to the design of a French architect, Boulanger. In front of its stands an equestrian statue of Theódoros Kolokotrónis, one of the heroes of the fight for Greek independence.

Hall of Honour
The entrance hall leads into a narrow Hall of Honour, with busts of King Otto and George I and busts and portraits of prominent figures in the fight for independence, as well as those of politicians (e.g. Ypsilántis, Miaoúlis, Kanáris, Kolokotrónis and a heroine of the struggle for independence, Bubulína). From this hall three doorways give access to the old Parliamentary chamber, in neo-classical style.

The Museum
The Museum occupies a series of rooms around the chamber, beginning on the left and continuing clockwise. The exhibits include pictures, weapons and uniforms ranging in date from Byzantine to modern times. Particular attention is devoted to the Orlov rising of 1770 and the war of Greek independence (1821–30), with relics of Byron (of particular interest), Patriarch Gregory IV, Prince Paul Bonaparte, Kapodistrias, King Otto and Queen Amalia. There is also material relating to the struggle for freedom on Crete (Arkádi monastery) and to more recent history including the Balkan Wars.

*The Olympieion, the temple of Olympian Zeus*

# *Olympieion                                                    C3

A temple to the supreme god of the Greek pantheon, who had previously been worshipped in the open air, was built by Peisistratos on this site at some time before 550 B.C. – a hundred years before the erection of the temple of Zeus at Olympia. It measured 30 by 60 m (100 by 200 ft) – rather smaller than the later Parthenon (see Acropolis). The site, to the SE of the Acropolis, then lay outside the city.

Peisistratos' sons Hippias and Hipparchos resolved to replace this temple by a gigantic new structure with a double colonnade (*dipteros*) measuring 41 by 107·75 m (135 by 354 ft), comparable with the temple of Hera built by Polykrates on the island of Samos.

Work on this building, which was to have 8×21 columns, was suspended after the expulsion of Hippias in 510 B.C. and it lay unfinished for almost 350 years, until about 175 B.C., when the Syrian king Antiochos IV commissioned a Roman architect, Cossutius, to complete it. The new temple was designed to have a double colonnade of 8×20 Corinthian columns, 17 m (55 ft) high, of Pentelic marble; but this temple, too, remained unfinished, and it was not completed for another 300 years, until about A.D. 130, when Hadrian had it finished in accordance with Cossutius' plan. Its construction had thus taken altogether 700 years.

The cella, which contained a statue of Hadrian as well as the cult image of Zeus, has disappeared, as have most of the 104 columns, to the making of which went no less than 15,500 tons

**Situation**
Leofóros Olgas

**Buses**
12/3

**Trolleybuses**
2, 12

**Opening times**
*Mon.–Sat. 9 a.m.–3 p.m.
Sun. 10 a.m.–3 p.m.

103

of marble. The surviving remains, however – the group of 13 columns and part of the entablature at the SE corner, two isolated columns on the S side and another column which collapsed in 1852 – are still of imposing grandeur. It is not certain whether the 13 SE columns belong to the Hellenistic building and the three on the S side to the Roman one, or whether they are all of Roman date.

The entrance to the site is in Leofóros Olgas. Near the entrance, in the old defensive ditch of Athens, are a number of column drums from the Peisistratid temple. Farther W are the remains of Roman baths and other buildings. Through the partly reconstructed propylon we enter the large rectangular temenos in which the temple lies. From the S wall of the temenos we can look down into an excavated area on a lower level in which, among other structures, the foundations of the temple of Apollo Delphinios and the large rectangle of the Panhellenion can be distinguished. They are among the many temples and shrines on the banks of the Ilissos, which flows through this area; others include the temple of Aphrodite in the gardens on the right bank of the stream, the Metroon and the shrine of Artemis Agrotera on the left bank. In Christian times a basilica was built here by the ancient Kallirhoe spring.

---

## Omónia Square (Platia Omonías)                                    B3

**Electric Railway**
Omónia station

**Bus**
70

**Trolleybuses**
1, 5

Omónia Square (the Square of Concord, *omonoías*) and its immediate surroundings are one of the busiest parts of Athens – busy in terms of traffic, commerce and tourism, with numerous offices, shops and hotels. In the centre of the square are gardens and a fountain; but around it tall modern blocks have almost completely displaced the low classical-style buildings of the 19th c., creating a cosmopolitan atmosphere in sharp contrast to the male society of the typical old Greek coffee-houses.

Additional traffic and business is brought to the square by its Electric Railway station and underground shopping arcade. Omónia Square was laid out by the town-planners of the 19th c. It was originally intended to be the site of the new royal palace which was finally built in Sýntagma Square (see Old Palace). From this square radiate two sides of the isosceles triangle which was the basis of the city plan – Pierós Street to the SW and two parallel streets, Panepistimíou and Stadíou Streets, to the SE. The third side of the triangle is formed by Ermoú Street, which is bisected by Athinás Street, running S from Omónia Square. A third of the way down Athinás Street is Kótzia Square, with the Town Hall and Head Post Office.

---

## Ómorphi Ekklisía

**Electric Railway**
Patissiá station

**Bus**
54

**Distance**
8 km (5 miles) N of city centre, in suburb of Galátsi

The Ómorphi Ekklisía or "Beautiful Church" is a 12th c. domed cruciform church which owes its name to its graceful proportions and its handsome exterior of carefully fitted dressed stone. In the 14th c. a chapel was built on to the S side and a painter of considerable quality, probably from Salonica, embellished the interior with fine frescoes, which were restored in 1957. (Key in the Byzantine Museum (see entry).)

## Pantánassa Church                                   C2

The church of the Pantánassa (the Mother of God, Protectress of All), also known as the Panayía Megálou Monastíriou, is all that remains of the 10th c. nunnery which gives Monastiráki Square its name. It is a three-aisled basilica, with three columns between the aisles and an elliptical dome over the central aisle. The interior is richly decorated but of little artistic interest.

**Situation**
Monastiráki Square

**Electric Railway**
Monastiráki station

**Buses**
10, 72

## Párnis

This range of limestone mountains rising to 1413 m (4636 ft) divides Attica on the N from Bogotia. In ancient times there was a sanctuary of Zeus the Rain-Bringer on the summit. Nowadays Mount Párnis attracts many visitors with its pine forests and its pleasant climate.

It is reached by way of the outlying suburb of Achárnes (see entry), starting-point of a road (12 km–7½ miles) which winds its way up with numerous sharp bends. After passing a sanatorium (alt. 1000 m – 3200 ft) the road comes in 2 km (1¼ miles) to the Ayía Triáda chapel, where there are a tourist pavilion and a hotel. Here the road divides: the right-hand branch leads to the Mount Parnes Casino (cableway), while to the left (3 km – 2 miles) is a mountain hut from which it is possible to climb to the summit.

**Bus**
116

**Cableway**

**Distance**
31 km (19 miles) N

## Peanía/Liopési

The village of Liopési occupies the site of ancient Paiania, the birthplace of Demosthenes (384 B.C.), and is thus also known as Peanía. It is now an agricultural centre. Its late Byzantine churches (Ayía Paraskeví, Ayía Triáda, etc.), with frescoes, are of a type found also at Markópoulo (10 km – 6 miles SE) and Korópi (6 km – 4 miles S). The Kanakis taverna is popular with visitors from Athens, particularly diplomats.

Stalactitic cave
A particular tourist attraction is the Koutoúki stalactitic cave on the E side of Hymettos (see entry), discovered in 1926, which can be reached from the village on an asphalted road. The cave, 500 m (1640 ft) above sea level, has an area of 3800 sq. m (40,000 sq. ft) and is indirectly lit.

**Bus**
44

**Distance**
20 km (12 miles) E

**Opening times**
Cave: Mon.–Sat. 10 a.m.–5.30 p.m., Sun. 9 a.m.–5.30 p.m.

## Pendéli Monastery

Pentélikon

## Pentélikon

The Pentélikon of Pendéli range (1109 m – 3639 ft) bounds the plain of Attica on the NE. Pentelic marble was used in the great classical buildings on the Acropolis (see entry) and in the

**Bus**
105

**Distance**
16 km (10 miles) NE

famous "Moschophoros" (Calf-Carrier) in the Acropolis Museum (see entry), and it is still being worked today.

Pendéli Monastery

Leaving Athens by way of Leofóros Kifissiás and going NE, we pass through the suburb of Chalándri and come in another 8 km (5 miles) to a village with a poplar-shaded square (restaurant) in which is Pendéli Monastery, founded in 1578 (alt. 430 m – 1410 ft). The monastery buildings are modern. In the basement, which is entered from outside, visitors are shown various sacred books and one of the "secret schools" in which monks taught children during the period of Turkish occupation.

A flight of steps to the right leads into the monastery courtyard with its beautiful little church and ranges of cells.

The road continues past the monastery to a square surrounded by cafés, where there is a small church set among trees. From here can be seen the marble quarries which disfigure the hill and the modern technical installations on the summit. Below the square, among the trees, is a little country house which belonged to the Duchesse de Plaisance; the house is now surrounded by modern bungalows (in Leofóros Dukíssis Plakentías).

Daou Pendéli Monastery

On the eastern slopes of Pentélikon is another monastery, Daou Pendéli. It is reached by leaving Athens on the Marathon road and turning left 21 km (13 miles) from the city centre. Daou Pendéli, founded in the 12th c. and rebuilt in the 16th, has been called "the only example of a large monastic establishment in Greece outside Athos" (Kirsten-Kraiker).

# Philopappos Monument

Hill of the Muses

# Phyle (Filí)

**Bus**
To Filí

**Distance.**
18 km (11 miles) NW
to village, then 10 km (6 miles)
to site

Phyle, like Panakton (on the old road from Athens to Thebes) and Dekeleia (near present-day Tatói, on the E side of Mount Párnis), was one of a ring of frontier fortresses built in the 4th c. B.C. to protect Attica against attack from the Megarid and Boeotia to the W.

The road from Athens runs via Anó Liossía to the village of Filí (terminus of bus) and continues NW past the Moní ton Klistón (4 km – 2½ miles – see entry). 6 km (4 miles) beyond the monastery, at the end of the asphalted road, the fortress of Phyle can be seen on the left.

Phyle stands in a rugged mountain setting on a rectangular plateau (alt. 683 m – 2241 ft), commanding the pass which carried the old road from Athens to Tanagra in Boeotia. The site had probably been occupied by an earlier fortress in which Thrasyboulos assembled his followers in 403 B.C. for the attack on the Thirty Tyrants. The W and SW parts of the 4th c. fortress (excavated by Skias in 1900) have collapsed into the gorge. Considerable stretches of the imposing walls of dressed stone have been preserved to the level of the wall-walk on the E and SE. The stones measure 2·75 m by 38 cm (9 ft by 1 ft 3 in).

# Piraeus (Pireéfs)

Piraeus (modern Greek Pireéfs) is the largest port in Greece, the starting-point of services to Europe and the Middle East and of most domestic services.

The Kastella hill (87 m – 275 ft) was already occupied in Neolithic times. It was fortified by Hippias in 512 B.C. and became the nucleus round which the town developed. The settlement, which had a sanctuary of Artemis Mounychia, acquired increased importance when Themistocles, as archon of Athens, made it the city's naval base (493–492 B.C.). The little bays of Zea and Mounychia to the E became the home of the new Athenian fleet, while the larger inlet to the W – known as the Kantharos from its shape, resembling an Attic drinking-cup – became the commercial harbour, as it still is today.

Themistocles surrounded the town with a wall which according to Thucydides had a total length of 60 stadia (11 km – 7 miles), and Pericles connected Piraeus with Athens by building the Long Walls. After the Persian wars the town walls were strengthened by Konon (394–391 B.C.). The town itself was laid out on a rectangular plan according to the system devised by Hippodamos of Miletus.

The town was destroyed by Sulla in 86 B.C. and thereafter was a place of no importance. In the Middle Ages it was known as Porto Leone after the two marble lions which flanked the entrance to the harbour. One of them now stands in front of the Arsenal in Venice: it bears a runic inscription scratched on it around 1040 by Varangians (the Scandinavian bodyguard of the Byzantine Emperors).

Piraeus recovered its importance after the liberation of Greece in the 19th c., when the modern town was laid out on a rectangular plan (by Schaubert) as the ancient one had been.

**Railway**
Terminus of State Railways, Athens
Electric Railway and Peloponnese Railway

**Buses**
70 (Omónia Square)
165 (Sýntagma Square)

**Shipping services**
To Greek islands

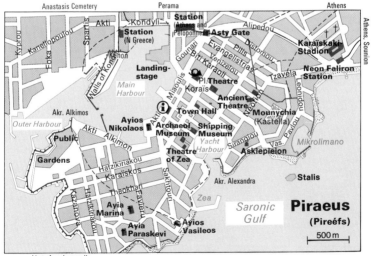

———— Line of ancient walls

*Piraeus: Greece's largest port*

Thereafter Piraeus soon displaced the port on the island of Syros which had hitherto been the principal shipping centre in this part of the Aegean.

In addition to the principal harbour of Kantharos the two smaller ancient harbours on the E side of the town – Bassalimáni (the ancient Zea) and Mikrolímano, formerly called Turkolímano (the ancient Mounychia) – are still in use. New port installations to relieve the pressure on Piraeus are being developed in Pháliron Bay, site of the earliest harbour of Athens before the foundation of Piraeus.

The most characteristic parts of the modern town, which combines the atmosphere of a large port with the amenities of a city, are around the principal harbour, in Korais Square on the higher ground between that harbour and Mikrolímano, and in the vicinity of Mikrolímano with its numerous tavernas.

Ancient remains

The remains of ancient boat-sheds can be seen under water in the two harbours on the E side, and behind the Archaeological Museum in Chariláou Trikoúpi Street (in course of reconstruction for many years) is a Hellenistic theatre (2nd c. B.C.). Stretches of Konon's town walls 394–391 B.C.) can be seen at the SW tip of the town.

Shipping Museum

At the S end of the Bassalimáni quay, where the old harbour of Zea adjoins the new Marina Zea, is a semicircular building housing an interesting Shipping Museum which covers the history of shipping from antiquity to modern times.

*The Pláka*

## Pláka                                                           C3

The Pláka, the older part of modern Athens, lies between the
northern slopes of the Acropolis (see entry) and Ermoú Street,
extending E almost to the Leofóros Amalías. In its narrow
streets and little squares are a number of small churches, from
the Metamórfosis (SW – see entry) to the Sotír tou Kottáki (E),
from Ayios Nikodímos (SW – see entry) to the Kapnikaréa (N –
see entry). It is a district of houses in neo-classical style, mostly
of modest size, with attractive tiled roofs. At 5 Thólou Street is
an old building (altered by Kleanthes) which housed the
University (see entry) before its move to Christian Hansen's
new building in Epistomíou Street. The building is now a
taverna.
The numbers of old houses and tavernas in the Pláka are,
unfortunately, being reduced all the time as the district is
increasingly taken over by the showier and noisier establishments which cater for the tourist trade, but there is still an
abundance of churches.

**Electric Railway**
Monastiráki station

**Buses**
10, 16, 93/10

**Trolleybuses**
1, 2, 5, 12
(stops in Filellínon Street)

## Pnyx                                                           C2

The Pnyx (110 m – 361 ft) is one of the range of three hills – the
others being the Hill of the Nymphs and the Hill of the Muses
(see entries) – to the SW of the Acropolis (see entry). After the
reform of Kleisthenes (508–507 B.C.) the Ekklesia, the popular

**Bus**
16

assembly of Athens, met here, before moving to the Theatre of Dionysos (see entry) in the 4th c. B.C. Here men like Themistocles addressed the people of Athens. There are remains of the rock-cut orators' platform, with the altar of Zeus (*c.* 400 B.C.) behind it; the retaining wall (*c.* 330 B.C.), built of huge blocks of stone, which supported the semicircular auditorium on the N; and the *diateichisma*, the wall built in 337 B.C. to shorten the line of the city's defences.

Along the W side are the rows of seating for the spectators of the *son et lumière* shows which now take place here.

# *Póros

**Boat services**
Argossaronikos service; connections with Galatás on the mainland, which is connected by bus with Nauplia

The island of Póros (area 23 sq. km – 9 sq. miles), the headquarters of the ancient Kalaurian league, and the ancient Kalaureia, is separated from the NE coast of the Peloponnese by a strait only 250 m (275 yd) wide. The town of Póros (pop. 4000) lies on a rocky promontory on the strait. The quiet bay to the W of the town is like an inland lake; and indeed the channels to the E and W are passable only by small boats.

There was a town here in Mycenaean times, on the site of the later temple of Poseidon. The temple enjoyed the right of sanctuary; and it was here that Demosthenes, the great advocate of resistance to the Macedonian hegemony, poisoned himself in 322 B.C. while fleeing from Antipatros. The ancient city was abandoned in Roman times; the present town was established only in the later medieval period.

Póros town

The town of Póros has a strikingly beautiful situation. The old Arsenal built by Kapodistrias now houses a Naval Training School. In front of it is moored the cruiser "Averoff", a boy's training ship.

Panayía Monastery

A road runs past the Naval School to the Panayía Monastery above the E coast (4 km (2½ miles): bus), which has a richly gilded iconostasis. Near the monastery are a number of tavernas with fine views over the sea.

Sanctuary of Poseidon

From the monastery it is a 45 minutes' uphill walk to the sanctuary of Poseidon (which can also be reached on an asphalted road from Póros). There are only scanty remains of the temple (6th c. B.C.), but the trip is worthwhile for the sake of the view over the sea to the island of Aegina.

From the sanctuary it is another 45 minutes' walk down through pine forests to the N coast with its beautiful bays.

Galatás/Troizen

An interesting trip can be made to Galatás on the mainland and from there to the remains of ancient Troizen (modern Greek Trizína), the setting of the myth of Hippolytos and Phaidra.

# Pórto Ráfti

**Bus**
To Pórto Ráfti

**Distance**
38 km (24 miles) E

Pórto Ráfti, a picturesque little port on the E coast of Attica, 9 km (6 miles) S of Brauron (see entry), is so called after a large marble statue of the Roman period, popularly known as the "Tailor" (*raftis*), on a rocky islet outside the harbour.

The predecessor of the present town in ancient times was Prasiai, on the hill of Koroni at the SE end of the bay, which played an important part in the shipping trade between Attica and the islands during the 7th and 6th c. B.C. The ancient town walls which can still be seen, however, date only from the 3rd c. B.C.

To the N of Pórto Ráfti bay was Steiria, to which a Mycenaean necropolis in the Peráti district belonged (finds in Brauron museum).

## *Rhamnoús

The ancient coastal town of Rhamnoús is reached from the village of Marathón (see entry) by way of Káto Soúli. Coming from the S, the road leads on to the terrace of the sanctuary of Themis and Nemesis, the goddesses of the legal order and of retribution.

Temple of Themis
This is a small Archaic temple in antis of polygonal grey limestone masonry, built around 500 B.C. and further embellished after the Persian wars. A cult figure by the sculptor Chairestratos (c. 280 B.C.) is in the National Archaeological Museum (see entry) in Athens (Room 29).

Temple of Nemesis
Immediately adjoining is the larger temple of Nemesis, for which Phidias or his pupil Agorakritos carved the cult image (c. 420 B.C.: fragments in National Archaeological Museum, Room 17). It is a Doric peripteral temple, built in marble, with 6 × 12 columns, begun about 430 B.C. but – as can be seen from the unfinished state of some of the columns – never completed. In front of the temple is the altar.

From the temple terrace there are beautiful far-ranging views over the site of the ancient town, now largely overgrown with macchia.

A footpath flanked by tombs runs down to the sea, above which rises the hill on which the acropolis was built. Remains of walls can be seen on the E side, and of a theatre on the seaward side.

**Buses**
To Marathón, Grammatikó and Soúli

**Distance**
52 km (32 miles) NE

**Opening times**
Sunrise to sunset

## Roman Agora                                                    C2

The Roman Agora or Market was laid out at the beginning of the Christian era immediately W of the Tower of the Winds (see entry), built some decades earlier. It was connected with the older Greek Agora to the W by a road which was discovered some years ago.

While the Greek Agora grew and developed over the centuries, this later market was laid out on a unified plan within a rectangular area measuring 112 by 96 m (365 by 315 ft). It has two gates: at the W end a Doric propylon built between 12 and 2 B.C. with an inscription recording that the market was dedicated to Athena Archegetes, and at the E end an Ionic

**Bus**
10

**Opening times**
At present closed

propylon probably dating from the reign of Hadrian (A.D. 117–138), when the adjoining Library of Hadrian (see entry) was also built.

Probably dating from the same period are the double-aisled colonnades of slender unfluted Ionic columns which surround the market, as well as the shops and offices which open off the colonnades. On the S side is a fountain.

Mosque

On the N side of the market is a mosque built in the 15th c. in honour of Sultan Mehmet the Conqueror (Fetiye Camii); it is known to the Greeks as the Market Mosque (Djami tou Staropazaroú) and now used as an archaeological store.

Medrese

To the E of the mosque is the doorway (inscriptions) of a Turkish medrese (Koranic school).

## Salamis Island

**Bus**
88 (Pérama)

**Ferry services**
From Pérama (50 daily);
from Néa Péramos, E of Mégara

**Distance**
15 km (9 miles) W

The island of Salamis, lying close to the mainland of Attica, shuts off the Bay of Eleusis (see entry), which can be entered only through two narrow channels. The famous naval battle of Salamis (480 B.C.) took place in the more easterly of these channels. This limestone island, with hills rising to 404 m (1325 ft) and a deeply indented gulf on the W side, has little arable land. It is now caught up in the rapid development of the Athens region.

Probably first settled by Phoenicians, Salamis took part in the Trojan War under its king Aias (Ajax), son of Telamon. Another of Telamon's sons, Teukros, was believed to be the founder of the town of Salamis in Cyprus, which he named after his native island. The island was conquered by Athens in the time of Solon or Peisistratos. The naval battle fought in September 480 in the narrow strait, in which the large Persian vessels were unable to manoeuvre, was a powerful vindication of Themistocles' strategy and heralded the splendid flowering of

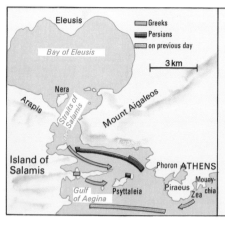

# Battle of Salamis

**27–28 September 480 B.C.**

With only 378 triremes against a Persian force of over 1200 vessels, the Athenian fleet was able to inflict a decisive defeat on the Persians thanks to the manoeuvrability of their ships, the local knowledge of their commanders and their skill in fighting at close quarters and to the Persian warships' inability to navigate in these narrow waters. The battle was watched by the Persian king Xerxes, seated on a golden throne on a hill near the coast. Cf. the account given by Aeschylus, who had himself taken part in the battle, in his drama "The Persians" (472 B.C.).

classical culture in the 5th c. Aeschylus took the battle as the theme of his topical tragedy "The Persians", which was performed in Athens for the first time eight years later, in 472 B.C.

The ferry from Pérama passes through the waters in which the battle took place while Xerxes watched from a throne set up on the mainland. 3 km (2 miles) W of the Paloukiá landing-stage, in the deep bay on the W side of the island, is the chief town, Salamis (pop. 12,000), with the church of Panayía tou Katharoú. 6 km (4 miles) W of the town is the Faneromení monastery, founded in 1661, in the building of which material from an ancient sanctuary was used. The church contains frescoes of 1735. The road continues to the NW tip of the island, where the ferry from Néa Péramos puts in.

## Schliemann's House                                    C3

This palatial mansion was built by Ernst Ziller in 1878–9 for Heinrich Schliemann, the discoverer of Troy and of Mycenaean culture, and his Greek wife Sophia. Its name, Ilíou Mélathron ("Palace of Ilion"), commemorated the excavation of Troy. Along the front of the building is a two-storey loggia with columns of Pentelic marble, with paintings in the vaulting. There are also wall paintings in the interior.

In the little garden to the left is a copy of Phidias' "Wounded Amazon".

The house is now occupied by the Areopagos, the Supreme Court of Appeal. A Schliemann Museum is planned.

**Situation**
Panepistimíou (Venizélou) Street

**Bus**
16

**Trolleybuses**
2, 3, 12

## *Soúnion

Every visitor to Athens should visit Cape Soúnion, not only for its magnificent sunsets but also for its famous temple of Poseidon, splendidly situated on the edge of a precipitous crag. Homer refers in the "Odyssey" (III, 278) to the "sacred cape" of Soúnion.

Temple of Poseidon
In the 7th c. B.C. there was probably a simple altar here; about 600 B.C. the large figures of kouroi now in the National Archaeological Museum (see entry) in Athens were set up beside it; and around 500 B.C. work began on the construction of a temple in grey-veined marble which was still unfinished when the Persians destroyed it in 480 B.C. On the substructure of this earlier temple the architect responsible for the temple of Hephaistos in Athens erected in 449 B.C. the present marble temple, with 6×13 exceptionally slender Doric columns. It stands on a terrace, artificially enlarged, to which a propylon gave access.

Boat-houses
In the bay below the temple were boat-houses, of which some remains can still be seen.

**Bus**
To Soúnion

**Distance**
68 km (42 miles) SE

**Opening times**
Mon.–Sat. 9 a.m.–sunset
Sun. 11 a.m.–sunset

*Cape Soúnion and the Temple of Poseidon*

Sanctuary of Athena

On a flat-topped hill NE of the temple (beyond the modern road) is a sanctuary of Athena of the 6th c. B.C. Beside a small building measuring only 5 by 6·80 m (16 by 22 ft), of which the lower courses of the walls and the base of a cult statue are preserved, are the foundations of a similar but larger temple (11·60 by 16·40 m (38 by 54 ft)), with the base of a cult statue. The roof was borne on four columns, in the fashion of a Mycenaean megaron. After suffering damage during the Persian wars the temple was rebuilt with two colonnades, not at the E and W ends as was the normal arrangement but at the E end and along the S side. The reason for this departure is a matter for conjecture.

## Stadion D4

**Situation**
Leofóros Ardíttou

**Buses**
12/3

**Trolleybuses**
2, 12

Ancient Stadion

The Stadion, also known as the Panathenaic Stadion, lies between two low hills NE of the Olympieion and SE of the National Garden (see entries). The present Stadion, built of marble, is the largest building in Athens, with seating for 70,000 spectators. Although entirely modern it has the same form and occupies the same site as its ancient predecessor, in which the Panathenaic games were held.

The ancient Stadion was built about 335 B.C. by the conservative politician Lykourgos, who also rebuilt the

*The Stadion: a modern structure on an ancient site*

Lykeion and the Theatre of Dionysos (see entry). 500 years later (A.D. 140–144) it was provided with new marble seating by Herodes Atticus. The track was 204 m (669 ft) long by 33·36 m (109 ft) wide. Four double herms from the ends of the track were recovered by excavation. The races were run over a distance of a stade or stadion (in Athens 178 m – 584 ft); in the two-stade race the runners turned at these herms.

Herodes Atticus, who was born in Marathon in A.D. 101 and died there in 177, was one of the great Maecenases of antiquity who rose to high dignities under Hadrian and Antoninus Pius. He was famous for his munificence, financing the Stadion and the Odeion (see entry) which bears his name in Athens, the renovation of the Stadion at Delphi, the provision of a water supply and the building of a nymphaeum at Olympia and the renovation of the spring of Peirene at Corinth.

In A.D. 133 Herodes Atticus erected on the hill of Ardettos, SW of the Stadion, a temple of Tyche, in which the members of the Heliaia (lawcourt) swore their annual oath. He also had his tomb built on the hill on the NE side of the Stadion; and the remains of a long structure found on the hill have been identified with this monument.

Although the Stadion was completely ruined and covered with earth and rubble its situation was known even before the excavation carried out by Ernst Ziller in 1869. Under the town plan drawn up by Schaubert and Kleanthes in 1832 Stadíou Street was intended to run straight from Omónia Square (see entry) to the Stadion instead of turning right into Sýntagma Square (see entry) as it does today. The plan was changed but the street name remained as it was.

Modern Stadion

When the Stadion was rebuilt for the first Olympic Games of modern times (1896) it was financed, as in the days of Herodes Atticus, by a wealthy private citizen, Yeoryios Averoff, who thus – like other modern Greeks, particularly those who have made their money abroad – continued the ancient tradition of the *euergetes* ("benefactor"). The modern Stadion, like the ancient one, has 47 tiers of seating and a rounded SE end, the *sphendone*.

## Stoa of Eumenes                                          C2

**Situation**
Dionysíou Areopagítou Street

**Bus**
16

**Opening times**
Mon.–Sat. 9 a.m.–6.30 p.m.
Sun. 10 a.m.–4.30 p.m.

Between the Odeíon of Herodes Atticus and the Theatre of Dionysos (see entries) is the Stoa of Eumenes, built by King Eumenes II of Pergamon (197–160 B.C.), who not only erected magnificent buildings in his own city (Great Altar of Pergamon) but sought also to do honour to Athens by the building of this stoa. His example was followed by his brother and successor Attalos II (160–139 B.C.), who built the Stoa of Attalos in the Agora (see entry), probably using the same architect.

The Stoa of Eumenes differed from the Stoa of Attalos, which it exceeded in length by 46 m (150 ft), in having no rooms behind the double-aisled hall. It was thus not designed for the purposes of business but was merely a spacious promenade for visitors to the temple and theatre of Dionysos. It was two-storeyed, with Doric columns on the exterior, Ionic columns in the interior on the ground floor and capitals of Pergamene type on the upper floor. Since the stoa was built against the slope of the hill, it was protected by a retaining wall supported by piers and round arches; the arcades, originally faced with marble, can still be seen.

In 1060, during the Byzantine period, the buildings on the southern slopes of the Acropolis were incorporated in the fortifications of the citadel, the Rizokastron. The defensive wall, coming from the Propylaia, took in the outer walls of the Odeíon of Herodes Atticus (see entry), the arcades of the Stoa of Eumenes and the walls of the *parodoi* of the Theatre of Dionysos.

In front of the E end of the Stoa of Eumenes are the foundations of the Monument of Nikias, erected in 320 B.C. to commemorate Nikias' victory as choregos. After its destruction by the Herulians in A.D. 267 material from this monument was built into the Beulé Gate of the Acropolis.

## Sýntagma Square (Platía Syntágmatos)                    C3

**Buses**
Numerous services (10, 16, etc.); trolleybuses 2, 3, 5, 12

Sýntagma Square (Platía Syntágmatos, Constitution Square), named after the constitution granted by King Otto on 3 September 1844, is the largest and most imposing square in Athens, the hub of the city's traffic and the starting-point of numerous bus services. In spite of this activity, however, the cafés in the centre of the square offer the opportunity for relaxation and refreshment. Around the square are numerous hotels and airline offices.

To the N, between Panepistimíou and Stadíou Streets, with two well-known cafés, Zonar's and Floka, there formerly stood the royal stables, on the site of a large ancient cemetery.

To the N the square rises towards the Old Palace (see entry), now occupied by the Greek Parliament, in front of which is a terrace with the Tomb of the Unknown Soldier. Every Sunday at 11.15 there is a ceremonial changing of the guard by the Evzones in their traditional kilt-like costumes. On the walls on either side are bronze tablets recording Greek victories in the struggle for freedom from 1821 onwards.

Tomb of the Unknown Soldier

Recent investigations have suggested that the Lykeion – the Aristotelian school of philosophy from which we derive the word lyceum – was in the area of Sýntagma Square and the National Garden (see entry).

Lykeion

## **Theatre of Dionysos                                                         C3

The Theatre of Dionysos is the oldest of the three architectural complexes on the southern slopes of the Acropolis (the others being the Odeion of Herodes Atticus and the Stoa of Eumenes – see entries).
In the 6th c. B.C. Peisistratos transferred the cult of Dionysos from Eleutherai in the Kithairon hills (on the old road to Thebes) to Athens, where accordingly the god was known as Dionysos Eleuthereus, and a temple was built to house the old cult image from Eleutherai. In association with the cult of

**Situation**
Dionysíou Areopagítou Street

**Bus**
16

**Opening times**
Mon.–Sat. 9 a.m.–6.30 p.m.,
Sat. 10 a.m.–4.30 p.m.

*Theatre of Dionysos: the auditorium (left) and a figure from the stage building (right)*

Dionysos – the god of drunkenness, of transformation, of ecstasy and the mask – the Theatre of Dionysos was built in a natural hollow on the slopes of the Acropolis. Nine building phases have been distinguished by Travlos, the first two dating from the 6th and 5th c.

The theatre and the temple precinct were separated about 420 B.C., when a pillared hall facing S was built, involving the removal of the old temple, built of limestone. The brown breccia foundations of this later temple can be seen to the S of the remains of the hall.

Theatre

About 330 B.C. the theatre's present stone tiers of seating were built. The 64 tiers (of which 25 survive in part), which could accommodate some 17,000 spectators, are divided into three sections by transverse gangways, and the lowest section is divided vertically into 13 wedges separated by stairways. In the front row are seats of honour inscribed with the names of the occupants; in the centre is the seat reserved for the priest of Dionysos Eleuthereus, decorated with reliefs and with post-holes in the ground pointing to the existence of a canopy. Behind the priest's seat, on a higher level, is a throne for the Emperor Hadrian (A.D.117–138).

The tiers of seating rise up to a point directly below the Acropolis rock, where the cuttings for the top rows can be seen. In the rock face is a cave, once sacred to Dionysos, which was given an architectural façade by Thrasyllos in 320–319 B.C.; it has a tripod above it symbolising his victory as *choregos*. The two columns above the cave are tripod bases dating from the Roman period. The cave is now occupied by a small chapel of the Panayía Spiliótissa (Mother of God of the Cave).

The orchestra is paved with marble slabs and is surrounded by a marble barrier to provide protection from the wild beasts which took part in shows in Roman times. The stage buildings to the S, like the rest of the theatre, were much rebuilt in later periods. Here there are striking reliefs of Dionysiac scenes, dating from the Roman period; according to the most recent theory they were re-used in an orators' platform of the 5th c. A.D.

The importance of the Theatre of Dionysos – of which there is a good general view from the S wall of the Acropolis – lies in the fact that it was built when tragedy was first being introduced, and indeed created, in Athens. This first drama was performed in 534 B.C., probably in the Agora (see entry), by Thespis, a native of Ikaria (now Dionysius – see entry), who travelled about in a waggon with his company. This early dramatic form, in which a single actor performed with a chorus, was the beginning of a development which led in the 5th c. – the period of pride and confidence after the Persian wars – to the brilliant flowering of Greek tragedy. The works of the three great Attic tragedians were first performed in the Theatre of Dionysos in celebration of the Dionysiac cult; and here Aeschylus – who had fought at Marathon as a hoplite and was proud to have this recorded on his tombstone – as well as Sophocles and Euripides appeared in person. Thus the Theatre of Dionysos became the birthplace and origin of the European theatre.

Odeion

To the E of the theatre stood the square Odeion built by Pericles, where new excavations are in progress. Famed as the finest concert hall in Greece, this was completed in 443 B.C. and rebuilt between 65 and 52 B.C. after its destruction by Sulla in 86 B.C.

## Themistoclean Walls – Long Walls

Until the Persian wars only the Acropolis (see entry) was surrounded by walls; but after the destruction of Athens by the Persians in 480 B.C. Themistocles had a wall built round the city. The work was done in great haste, using the ruins of the monuments and buildings which had been destroyed.

A considerable stretch of these Themistoclean walls, with two gates (the Dipylon and the Sacred Gate), has been brought to light in the Kerameikos, another section N of the Olympieion (see entries). Further remains of the walls were found during the construction of the government buildings over the church of the Ayía Dýnamis (see entry) in Mitropóleos Street, at 6–8 Dragatsaníou Street (see Klafthmónos Square) and on the site of the Divani Zafolia Hotel, in Parthenónos Street, to the S of the Acropolis. These two latter sections are open to the public.

Themistoclean Walls

The city's defences were strengthened between 465 and 460 B.C. by the construction of the Long Walls, which ran SW and S from Athens and were designed to secure communications between Athens and the ports of Piraeus (see entry) and Phaleron. The road to Piraeus was further protected by a parallel wall built by Pericles in 445 B.C.

Long Walls

This defensive system was completed in 337 B.C. by the construction of the Diateichisma, an intermediate wall between the Hill of the Nymphs and the Hill of the Muses (see entries) which shortened the defensive line.

Diateichisma

## Thorikós

11 km (7 miles) N of Cape Soúnion (see entry) and 2 km (1¼ miles) N of Lávrion, near the coast (to the E of the road), is the site of ancient Thorikós, on a hill overlooking the bay of Lávrion, which was fortified in 490 B.C. to provide defence against Persian attack.
There was a settlement here in Mycenaean times, as is shown by two nearby tholos tombs (between the two summits of the hill and on its eastern slopes).
The most notable structure on the site is the theatre (5th–4th c. B.C.), which belonged to a sanctuary of Dionysos. It is of rather archaic type, with an orchestra which is neither circular nor semicircular, as was the usual style, but almost rectangular. In consequence the auditorium also departs from the usual circular form.

**Bus**
To Lávrion

**Distance**
79 km (49 miles) SE

## *Tower of the Winds (The Creek of Andronicos)     C3

The Tower of the Winds stands in the Pláka below the N side of the Acropolis (see entries). In the planning of the modern city of Athens in the 19th c. Eólou Street, named after the wind god Aiolos, was aligned directly on the tower, which forms a landmark at its southern end. Built about 40 B.C., the tower is an

**Situation**
At S end of Eólou Street (Pláka)

**Bus**
10

*Tower of the Winds and Roman Agora*

**Opening times**
At present closed

octagonal structure 12 m (40 ft) high, with sundials on the external walls; it originally housed a water-clock. Around the top runs a frieze with reliefs representing the eight wind gods – the beardless Notos, pouring out rain from an urn (S); Lips, holding the stern ornament of a ship (SW); Zephyros, a youth scattering flowers (W); Skiron the bringer of snow (NW); the bearded Boreas, blowing into a shell (N); Kaikias, also bearded, the bringer of hail (NE); Apeliotes, a young man bearing ears of corn and fruit (E); and Euros, wrapped in a cloak (SE). Photograph, above.

To the S of the tower is a building of the Roman period (1st c. A.D.) with the springing points of arches. Its function is uncertain (office of the market police, Caesareum?).

Adjoining the entrance to the excavated area is a marble latrine with seating for nearly 70.

To the W of the Tower of the Winds is the Roman Agora (see entry).

---

## *University – Academy – National Library    B3

**Situation**
Panepistimíou (Venizélou) Street

**Bus**
50

These three buildings in Panepistimíou (University) Street – now officially Venizélou Street – together with the New Palace (see entry), are the most striking achievements of the young kingdom of Greece in the field of architecture and town planning. The three buildings were designed by the Hansen brothers of Copenhagen.

*Architecture of the young kingdom of Greece: the University . . .*

*. . . and the Academy of Sciences*

**Trolleybuses**
1, 2, 3, 5, 12

University

The University, a plain neo-classical building with restrained ornament, was built in 1839–41 by Christian Hansen (1803–83). Behind the columns of the portico, above the doorway, is a representation of King Otto, who initiated the project, surrounded by Muses. In front of the entrance are figures of Kapodistrias, who as Governor of Greece (1827–31) proclaimed the foundation of the University, the writer and scholar Adamantios Korais (1748–1833) and also W. M. Gladstone. Immediately in front of the façade are statues of the poet Rigas Pherraios and Patriarch Gregory IV, who were murdered by the Turks in 1789 and 1821 respectively.

Academy

The two flanking buildings were designed by Christian Hansen's younger brother Theophil (1813–91) in a richer style. The design for both buildings was prepared in 1859, and work began in that year on the Academy of Sciences (to right of the University), which was financed by a Greek living in Vienna, Baron Sina. The building was not completed, however, until 1885.

National Library

The complex was completed when Theophil Hansen built the National Library, to the left of the University, in 1887–91.

# Záppion

See National Garden

# Practical Information

## Airlines

All the principal airlines have offices in Athens, mostly concentrated in and around Sýntagma Square.

Olympic Airways,
Leofóros Sýngrou, tel. (01) 92 92/1

British Airways,
10 Othonos Street, tel. (01) 3 25 06 01

Sightseeing tours (see entry)                              Charter flights

## Airport (aerodrómion)

Athens' airport of Hellenikon (Ellinikón) is 12 km ($7\frac{1}{2}$ miles)      Hellenikon
from the city centre on the road to the coast (Cape Soúnion).
There are two terminals – the eastern for all international
services, the western for the domestic services of Olympic
Airways.

There is a bus service between the airport and the city centre,      Airport buses
near Sýntagma Square, from 6 a.m. to midnight. There are
buses every 20 minutes. The journey takes half an hour.

## Air services (domestic)

Olympic Airways have a comprehensive network of services
connecting Athens with the following places:

| | |
|---|---|
| Alexandroúpolis | Kos |
| Chaniá (Crete) | Límnos |
| Chios | Mýkonos |
| Corfu (Kérkyra) | Mytilíni (Lesbos) |
| Ioánnina | Rhodes |
| Iráklion (Crete) | Salonica (Thessaloniki) |
| Kalamáta | Sámos |
| Kastoriá | Santoríni |
| Kaválla | Skiáthos |
| Kefallinía | Zákynthos |

There are also services in smaller aircraft – the Skyvan (18
seats) or Islander (9 seats) – from Athens to Mílos, Kýthira and
Sparta.

## Antiques (archaiótetes)

Antiques can be found in the shopping area around Sýntagma
Square, particularly between Stadíou and Panepistimíou

Streets, and in Pandrósou Street near Monastiráki Square. The export of Greek antiquities is strictly forbidden.

## Art and architecture

### The Greek temple

The temple, along with the theatre, is the most characteristic achievement of ancient Greek architecture. It is conceived not as a place of assembly for the faithful but as a shrine housing the cult image of the divinity. Its form is derived from the megaron, the principal room in a Mycenaean palace or house.

*Temple in antis*

The simplest type is the *temple in antis*, in which the naos (cella) has an entrance portico (pronaos) enclosed between projections of the side walls (antae). Between the antae are two columns supporting the pediment. Example: Treasury of the Athenians, Delphi.

In a *double anta temple* the rear end has a similar portico.

*Prostyle, amphiprostyle*

Where there is another row of columns in front of a temple in antis, supporting a projecting pediment (one column in front of each of the antae, with either two or four between), this is known as *prostyle* (E temple, Erechtheion). Where the rear end is similarly treated the temple is *amphiprostyle* (Temple of Athena Nike, Acropolis).

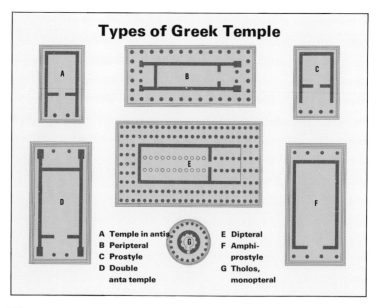

# Types of Greek Temple

A  Temple in antis
B  Peripteral
C  Prostyle
D  Double
   anta temple
E  Dipteral
F  Amphi-
   prostyle
G  Tholos,
   monopteral

From the second half of the 7th c. B.C. the classical type was the *peripteral* temple, in which the cella was surrounded by a line of columns (*peristasis*) on all four sides, with a pronaos forming the entrance and an opisthodomos at the rear end. The 6th c. showed a preference for an elongated plan with 6 × 16 columns (Temple of Hera, Olympia) or 6 × 15 (Temple of Apollo, Delphi). The classical proportions were achieved in the 5th c., with the columns along the sides numbering one more than twice the number at the ends – 6 × 13 in the Temple of Zeus at Olympia, 8 × 17 in the Parthenon of Athens.

Peripteral

Where there is a double row of columns round the four sides of a temple this is known as *dipteral* (Olympieion, Athens). Where the inner row is omitted to leave more room for the cella the temple is *pseudo-dipteral* (Temple of Artemis, Magnesia on the Maeander).

Diptéral

The tholos is a temple with a circular ground plan (Epidauros, Delphi).

Tholos

## The classical orders

The architecture of the Doric temple shows features derived from earlier timber-built structures. The shaft of the column, which tapers towards the top and has between 16 and 20 flutings, stands directly, without any special base, on the stylobate, the top step of the three-stepped base of the temple. There is a slight swelling (entasis), often barely perceptible, half-way up the column to relieve the rigidly geometrical effect. The capital consists of a convex moulding, the echinus, bearing the square abacus. Each pair of capitals supports one element of the architrave, the lowest part of the entablature. Above this is the frieze, made up of alternating triglyphs (projecting members with two vertical channels) and metopes, rectangular panels which may be either plain or carved in relief; and above this again is the triangular tympanon, framed in a cornice (geison) and usually containing sculptured figures. The sculptural decoration is found principally on the pediment and the metopes but may also extend to the front of the pronaos. Where a temple was built of limestone rather than marble it was faced with a coat of stucco. The stone was not left in its natural colouring but was painted, the predominant colours being blue, red and white.

Doric order

The Ionic order shows a preference for slenderer and softer forms than the Doric, which was always regarded as the "male" order. The flutings of the shaft are separated by blunt fillets. The column stands on a base, which may be either of the Asiatic type (with several horizontal flutings) or the Attic type (with an alternation between the convex torus and the concave trochilus moulding). The characteristic feature of the capital is the curving volute on either side. The architrave is not plain but is triply divided and stepped. The frieze is continuous, not divided into sections by triglyphs. The Ionic temple, developed in the territory of the Ionian Greeks, was well adapted to the construction of temples of very large size, such as those on Samos and in Asia Minor (Ephesos, Sardes, Didyma).

Ionic order

## Practical Information

**Corinthian order**

The Corinthian order is similar to the Ionic order except in its capitals. The characteristic feature of the Corinthian capital is the cluster of acanthus leaves which surround the circular body of the capital. The Corinthian order was much favoured during the Roman Imperial period, when a "composite" capital was also evolved, combining Ionic and Corinthian features, and decorative systems grew steadily richer and more elaborate.

# Churches

The first church buildings were erected in the 4th c., when Christianity became an officially recognised religion.

**Basilica**

The predominant form in these early years was the basilica, with one or two lower aisles on either side of the nave. The church is "oriented": i.e. the end containing the altar, marked by an apse, is to the E. The entrance is at the W end, which is preceded by a narthex and often by an atrium as well.
This type is found throughout the whole of the Roman Empire, from Rome to Jerusalem.

**Domed cruciform church**

In the 9th c. a new type of church, on a centralised plan, was developed in Greece – the domed cruciform church. Thereafter this became the predominant type.
The central dome is borne either on pendentives or on columns (occasionally on two pendentives and two columns). It may span only the main nave (as at Kaisarianí) or – borne on eight piers – both the nave and the aisles (as at Dafní).
The chancel is separated from the rest of the church by a stone screen, which later develops into the iconostasis. On either side are two small rooms for liturgical purposes, the prothesis and diakonikon. In consequence the E end of the church usually has three apses. The narthex at the W end is often preceded by an exonarthex or outer narthex.
The interior is painted in accordance with a strict iconographical system reflecting the heavenly hierarchy. The exterior is of undressed stone and brick, often in elaborate patterns. In the post-Byzantine period churches of basilican type were occasionally built – usually small, either aisleless or three-aisled.

# Technical terms

**Abacus**

The upper part of the capital of a Doric column, a square slab above the echinus. See diagram opposite.

**Abaton**

The innermost sanctuary of a temple, to which only priests were admitted.

**Acanthus**

A spiny-leaved plant used in the decoration of Corinthian and Byzantine (Justinianic) capitals.

**Acropolis**

The highest part of a Greek city; the citadel.

**Acroterion**

A figure or ornament on a roof ridge or the top of a pediment.

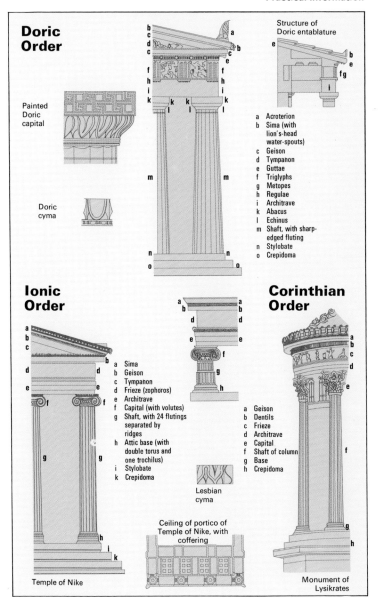

# Doric Order

Painted Doric capital

Doric cyma

Structure of Doric entablature

a Acroterion
b Sima (with lion's-head water-spouts)
c Geison
d Tympanon
e Guttae
f Triglyphs
g Metopes
h Regulae
i Architrave
k Abacus
l Echinus
m Shaft, with sharp-edged fluting
n Stylobate
o Crepidoma

# Ionic Order

a Sima
b Geison
c Tympanon
d Frieze (zophoros)
e Architrave
f Capital (with volutes)
g Shaft, with 24 flutings separated by ridges
h Attic base (with double torus and one trochilus)
i Stylobate
k Crepidoma

Lesbian cyma

Ceiling of portico of Temple of Nike, with coffering

Temple of Nike

# Corinthian Order

a Geison
b Dentils
c Frieze
d Architrave
e Capital
f Shaft of column
g Base
h Crepidoma

Monument of Lysikrates

## Practical Information

| | |
|---|---|
| Adyton | See Abaton. |
| Aegis | The cuirass worn by the goddess Athena, with the head of Medusa. |
| Agon | Contest, fight. |
| Agora | The market-place of a Greek city, the main centre of public life. |
| Amphiprostyle | (Temple) with columned portico at both ends. |
| Amphora | Two-handled jar of bulbous form. |
| Anathema | Votive offering. |
| Annulus | A ring round the shaft of a Doric column below the echinus. |
| Anta | A projection at the end of the side wall of a temple cella. |
| Apse | A projection, usually semicircular, at the end of a temple cella or church. |
| Architrave | A horizontal stone lintel resting on the columns of a temple, etc. See diagram, p. 127. |
| Archon | The highest official of a Greek city. |
| Astragal | Knucklebone; applied to the beaded moulding of the Ionic order. |
| Basileus | King. |
| Basilica | 1. Originally a royal hall (*stoa basilike*), usually divided into aisles, used for commercial or judicial purposes.<br>2. The standard form of Christian church developed in the 4th c., with three or five aisles. |
| Bema | 1. Platform used by orators.<br>2. Chancel of a Christian church. |
| Bomos | Square altar. |
| Bothros | Pit for offerings. |
| Bouleuterion | Council chamber; the meeting-place of the council (*boule*) of a Greek city. |
| Capital | The top of a column or pillar. |
| Caryatid | A female figure supporting an entablature. |
| Cavea | The auditorium (seating) of a theatre. |
| Cella | The enclosed chamber of a temple. |
| Cenotaph | Funerary monument not containing a body. |
| Chiton | A pleated linen garment worn with a belt, mostly in Ionia. |

| | |
|---|---|
| A short cloak. | Chlamys |
| "Choir-leader": a person who financed the choir performing in a tragedy. | Choregos |
| (Divinities) of the earth. | Chthonian |
| A semicircular niche surmounted by a half-dome. | Conch |
| Three-stepped platform of a temple. See diagram, p. 127. | Crepidoma |
| (Walls) of large irregular blocks. | Cyclopean |
| Wave moulding with double curvature. | Cyma |
| People, community; popular assembly; settlement. | Demos |
| Room to the right of the apse in a Byzantine church. | Diakonikon |
| Gangway between tiers of seating in a theatre. | Diazoma |
| (Temple) surrounded by a double row of columns. | Dipteral |
| Double gateway. | Dipylon |
| Passage; specifically, passage leading into a Mycenaean tholos tomb. | Dromos |
| Convex moulding under the abacus of a Doric capital. See diagram, p. 127. | Echinus |
| The superstructure (of a temple, etc.) carried by columns. | Entablature |
| Swelling in the lower part of a column for optical effect. | Entasis |
| A youth who is not yet a full citizen. | Ephebe |
| See Architrave. | Epistyle |
| Ceremonial pall. | Epitaphios |
| Inner narthex (porch) of a church. | Esonarthex |
| A recess or projection, usually semicircular, containing benches. | Exedra |
| Outer narthex (porch) of a church. | Exonarthex |
| Decorative band above the architrave of a temple. | Frieze |
| Cornice. See diagram, p. 127. | Geison |
| Fight between gods and giants. | Gigantomachia |
| A school for physical training or general education, consisting of a square or rectangular courtyard surrounded by colonnades and by rooms of varying size and function. | Gymnasion |
| A temple 100 feet long. | Hekatompedon |

## Practical Information

| | |
|---|---|
| Heraion | Temple or sanctuary of Hera. |
| Herm | A square pillar with a head of Hermes or some other god; later with a portrait head. |
| Heroon | Shrine of a hero. |
| Hieron | Sanctuary. |
| Hierophant | Priest of the mysteries (i.e. at Eleusis). |
| Himation | Cloak worn over the chiton. |
| Hoplite | Heavily armed foot soldier. |
| Hydria | Water jar. |
| Hypocaust | Under-floor heating system for baths, etc. |
| Hypostyle | Having a roof supported by columns. |
| Iconostasis | Screen in a Byzantine church between the sanctuary and the rest of the church, bearing tiers of icons. |
| Kathedra | Bishop's throne. |
| Katholikon | Principal church of a monastery. |
| Klepsydra | Well-house, cistern; water-clock. |
| Kore (plural korai) | Maiden, girl; statue of a girl. |
| Kouros (plural kouroi) | Youth; statue of a naked youth. |
| Krepidoma | Three-stepped platform of a temple. |
| Lapiths | A legendary people in Thessaly. |
| Lekythos | Narrow-necked oil flask. |
| Maeander | A continuous fret or key pattern. |
| Megaron | The principal room in a Mycenaean palace or house. |
| Metope | Rectangular panel between the triglyphs in the frieze of a Doric temple, either plain or with relief decoration. |
| Metroon | Sanctuary of the Mother of the Gods. |
| Monopteral | (Temple) without a cella, usually circular. |
| Naiskos | Small temple. |
| Naos | Cella of temple. |
| Narthex | Porch of a Byzantine church. |
| Necropolis | Cemetery. |

| | |
|---|---|
| Shrine of the nymphs; fountain-house. | Nymphaion |
| Hall (usually roofed) for theatrical performances. | Odeion |
| Wine-jug. | Oinochoe |
| Sanctuary of Olympian Zeus. | Olympieion |
| Chamber at the rear end of a temple. | Opisthodomos |
| Circular or semicircular area between the stage and auditorium of a theatre in which the chorus danced. | Orchestra |
| Large block of stone, set vertically, in the bottom course of a temple wall. | Orthostat |
| A system of voting on potsherds (*ostraka*) for the banishment of a citizen. | Ostracism |
| "All Holy"; the Mother of God, Mary. | Panayia |
| "Ruler of All"; Christ. | Pantocrator |
| Triangular termination of a ridged roof. | Pediment |
| A triangular section of vaulting forming the transition from a square base to a circular dome. | Pendentive |
| A woollen cloak worn by women. | Peplos |
| Enclosure wall of a sacred precinct. | Peribolos |
| (Temple) surrounded by a peristyle. | Peripteral |
| See peristyle. | Peristasis |
| Colonnade surrounding a building. | Peristyle |
| Large storage jar. | Pithis |
| Military leader. | Polemarch(os) |
| (Masonry) of irregularly shaped stones. | Polygonal |
| A kind of limestone. | Poros |
| Seat of honour in a theatre or stadion. | Prohedria |
| Entrance portico of temple. | Pronaos |
| Monumental form of propylon. | Propylaia |
| Gateway. | Propylon |
| Fore-stage. | Proskenion |
| (Temple) with columned portico in front. | Prostyle |
| Room to left of apse in a Byzantine church. | Prothesis |

## Practical Information

| | |
|---|---|
| Protome | Human torso or forequarters of animal as a decorative feature on a building or vase. |
| Pyrgos | Tower, bastion. |
| Rhyton | Drinking vessel, often in the form of an animal's head. |
| Sima | Gutter of building, with lion's-head water-spouts. |
| Skene | Stage building of theatre. |
| Sphendone | Rounded end of stadion. |
| Spira | Rounded base of cella wall. |
| Stadion | 1. Measure of length, 600 feet.<br>2. Running track 600 feet long.<br>3. Running track, stadium, with embankments or benches for spectators. |
| Stele | Upright stone slab (often a tombstone), usually with an inscription and frequently with relief carving. |
| Stoa | Portico; hall with pillars along front. |
| Strigil | Curved blade used to scrape dust and oil off the body after exercise. |
| Stylobate | The uppermost step of a temple platform. See diagram, p. 127. |
| Synthronon | Stone benches for clergy in the apse of a Byzantine church. |
| Temenos | Sacred precinct. |
| Templon | Chancel screen in Byzantine church. |
| Tetrastyle | (Temple) with four columns on façade. |
| Thesauros | Treasury. |
| Tholos | Circular building, rotunda; domed Mycenaean tomb. |
| Thymele | Altar in orchestra of theatre. |
| Toreutics | The art of ornamental metalwork. |
| Torus | Convex moulding of semicircular profile. See diagram, p. 127. |
| Triglyph | Projecting member, with two vertical channels, between metopes of the Doric order. See diagram, p. 127. |
| Trochilus | Convex moulding. See diagram, p. 127. |
| Tympanon | Rear wall of temple pediment. See diagram, p. 127. |
| Volute | Spiral scroll of Ionic capital. |
| Xoanon | Archaic wooden cult image. |

## Banks (trápeza)

Banks are open Monday to Friday 8.30 a.m.–1.30 p.m.
The Bank of Greece branch at Ellinikón airport is open day and night.

## Bathing

Although Athens has its public swimming pools, both indoor and open-air, and some hotels also have pools, visitors are more likely to be interested in the facilities for sea bathing.
There are no bathing beaches in Athens itself or in Piraeus, but there are very many beaches and bathing resorts on the "Apollo Coast" between Athens and Soúnion (at Soúnion itself and at Glyfáda, Voúla, Vouliagméni, Várkitsa and Lagonísi) and on the E coast in the Marathon area (Schiniás, Paralía Marathónos, Néa Mákri, Máti).

## Bicycle hire (prodílato)

If it is not too hot, cycling can be a pleasant way of sightseeing in Athens. Bicycles can be hired from the following firms:
Zenetos, Kifissias 278 (Kifissia Square), tel. 8 08 08 13.
Babalis, St Kerkyra 65, Kypseli, tel. 8 22 18 47.
Kalfopoulos, Markora 52, tel. 2 01 97 80.

## Boat hire

Information about the hire of boats and yachts can be obtained from the Association of Yacht Brokers, 34–36 Alkionis Street, Paleó Fáliro, tel. 9 81 65 82.

## Bookshops (bibliopolía)

English bookshops

Atlantis, 8 Korai Street, near the Academy.
Cacoulides, 39 Panepistimíou (Venizélou) Street, near the Academy.
Eleftheroudakis, 4 Nikís Street, near Sýntagma Square.
Kaufmann, 28 Stadíou Street, near Klafthmónos Square; 11 Voukourestíou Street, near Sýntagma Square.
Pantelides, 11 Amerikís Street, near the Academy.

## Camping

Camping outside recognised camping sites is prohibited in Greece. The following is a selection of camping sites in the Athens area:

Athens Camping Ground, 198 Athinón Street, Peristéri, tel. 5 71 53 26.

## Practical Information

Balkan Tourist, on the national highway to Lamia, tel. 8 01 58 21.
19 km (12 miles) from city centre, at Néa Kifissiá.

Dafní, Ierá Odós, tel. 5 90 95 27.
10 km (6 miles) from city centre.

Néon Evropaikón Camping Ground, Néa Kifissiá, tel. 8 01 64 35.
16 km (10 miles) from city centre on the Lamia road.

Néa Mákri Camping Ground, 156 Marathónos Street, tel. 02 94–927 19.

Soúnion Camping Ground, tel. 02 92–3 93 58.
6 km (4 miles) from Soúnion.

Information about camping sites can be obtained from the ELPA offices in Athens, at 2–4 Messógion Street.

# Car hire

There are numerous car hire firms in Athens and Piraeus. An international driving licence is necessary. Tariffs vary according to the type of car, the duration of the hire and the time of year.

Avis, Leofóros Amalías 48, tel. 32 24 95 1–2.

Driver, Leofóros Sýngrou 12, tel. 92 17 50 3–5, 9 21 55 03.

Helios, 138 Solonos Street, tel. 3 63 11 24.

Hertz, 3 Filellínon Street.

International Car Rental, Leofóros Sýngrou 35, tel. 9 23 50 65.

# Chemists

There are numerous chemists' shops in Athens. They can be identified by a cross on a round plate above the entrance and the word *ΦAPMAKEION*.

Opening times

Chemists' opening times vary over the year. They are normally as follows:
Summer: Mon.–Sat. 8.30 a.m.–1.30 p.m. (2.30 p.m.); Tues., Thurs. and Fri. 5.30–8.30 p.m.
Winter: Mon.–Sat. 8.30 a.m.–1.30 p.m.; Tues., Thurs. and Fri. 4.30–7.30 p.m.

Emergency service

Every chemist's shop displays a notice giving the address of the nearest chemist on the emergency roster.

The "Athens News" also lists, under the heading "Chemists – Pharmacies", chemists open at night and on Sundays and public holidays.
In emergency dial 100.

## Church services

There are services in English in the following churches:

St. Paul's Anglican Church, 29 Filellínon Street, tel. 71 49 06.    Church of England

St Denis Cathedral, Leofóros Panepistimíou, tel. 3 62 36 03 and 3 60 66 55.    Roman Catholic

St Andrew's American Church, 66 Sina Street, tel. 7 70 74 48.    Interdenominational

## Climate

The climate of Athens and Attica is at its best for the visitor in spring and autumn. The months of March, April and May are mild, and nature is at its greenest and gayest. The summer months are very hot, particularly in the city. In September the temperature falls to a more agreeable level, and the first showers of rain may fall in October.
Average temperatures in Athens are as follows (°C/°F):

| | | | | | |
|---|---|---|---|---|---|
| Jan. | 9·3/48·7 | Feb. | 10/50 | Mar. | 11·4/54 |
| Apr. | 13·4/60 | May | 20·2/68·4 | June | 24·7/76·5 |
| July | 27·5/81·5 | Aug. | 27·5/81·5 | Sept. | 24·6/76·3 |
| Oct. | 18·8/65·8 | Nov. | 14·9/58·8 | Dec. | 11·1/52 |

## Currency

The Greek unit of currency is the drachma, which is divided into 100 lepta. There are banknotes for 50, 100, 500 and 1000 dr. and coins in denominations of 5, 10, 20 and 50 lepta and 1, 2, 5, 10 and 20 dr.    Unit of currency

Visitors may take into Greece a maximum of 1500 dr. in Greek currency. There are no restrictions on the import of foreign currency either in the form of cash or of travellers' cheques.    Import of currency

Visitors may take out a maximum of 1500 dr. in Greek currency. Foreign currency up to 500 US dollars may be taken out again within a year; larger amounts may be taken out if they have been declared on entry.    Export of currency

It is advisable to take money in the form of travellers' cheques or to use a Eurocard. The principal credit cards are widely accepted in larger towns.    Travellers' cheques, etc.

# Customs regulations

Import

Visitors to Greece can import without payment of duty items required for their personal use and gifts up to a value of 150 US dollars. They may also take in, duty-free, 200 cigarettes (or 50 cigars or 200 g of tobacco), one bottle of spirits, up to 10 kg of sweets, one bottle of perfume, one bottle of eau-de-cologne, a camera and films, a cine-camera and projector, a pair of binoculars, a portable radio, a record-player with up to 20 records, a tape-recorder, a portable typewriter, a bicycle and sports and camping equipment. These last items must be entered on the visitor's passport.
The import of flowers and plants, and also of radio transmitters, is prohibited.

Export

Visitors may take out provisions for the journey up to a value of 50 dollars and souvenirs up to a value of 150 dollars. The export of antiquities and works of art is prohibited except in exceptional cases.
Items brought in for a visitor's personal use must be taken out again.

# Dental emergency service

Elpis Hospital, tel. 6 43 00 01 (operates from 10 p.m. to 6 a.m.).

# Electricity

220 V AC; on ships frequently 110 V.

# Embassies

United Kingdom

1 Ploutárchou Street,
tel. (01) 73 62 11.

United States of America

Leofóros Vas. Sofías 91,
tel. (01) 71 29 51, 71 84 01.

Canada

4 Ioannou Gennadioú Street,
tel. (021) 73 95 11–8.

# Emergency telephone numbers

Tourist Police

The most useful source of assistance for the tourist is the Tourist Police, tel. 171.

Fire

In case of fire dial 199.

Other emergency numbers

See last page.

# Events

There are three English-language periodicals which give
information about entertainments and other events in Athens:
"The Athenian" (monthly)
"The Week in Athens" (weekly)
"Time In" (monthly)

Some major events:

| | |
|---|---|
| Carnival with parades in the Pláka. | February–March |
| Son et lumière (see under Theatres, below). | April–October |
| Folk dancing in Philopappos Theatre. | May–September |
| Athens Festival, with performances of ancient dramas, operas, music and dancing in Odeion of Herodes Atticus (until September). Wine festivals (e.g. at Dafní). | July |
| Performances in Lykabettos Theatre (throughout the summer); performances by Lyric Theatre in Odeion of Herodes Atticus (throughout the summer: in winter in Olympia Theatre, 59 Akadimías Street). | Summer season |
| Folk dancing by the Greek Lyceum in Aliki Theatre, 2 Amerikís Street. | November–March |

# Ferry services (féribot)

There are two important ferry services in Attica:
Pérama–Salamis: 60 sailings daily.
Oropós (northern Attica)–Erétria (Euboea): 35 sailings daily.

# Food and drink

Greek hotels provide a mainly international cuisine, given
added colour by Greek dishes and garnishings. In restaurants
(estiatório, tavérna, restorán), rotisseries (psistariá) and the
more modest inns (pandochion) the native Greek cuisine
predominates. This shows Oriental (mainly Turkish) influence,
with much use of olive oil, garlic and herbs.
 
Greek cuisine

The menu is frequently written in English as well as Greek, but
in the more modest establishments it is usually only in Greek,
and probably written by hand. It is quite normal, however,
except in restaurants of the higher categories, to go into the
kitchen and choose your meal there.

The breakfast (próyevma) provided in hotels is usually of
normal continental type. Lunch (yévma) is normally served
between noon and 3 p.m., dinner (dípno) between 8 and 10
p.m.
 
Meal-times

# Practical Information

The Greek menu offers a varied range of dishes. Much use is made of fresh vegetables. The following is a selection of the most popular dishes:

**Hors d'œuvre (orektiká)**

There is a wide choice. In addition to the appetisers (meze) served with the aperitif the range includes prawns, seafood, stuffed vine-leaves (dolmádes) and salads (salátes).

**Soups (soúpes)**

Greek soups are usually very substantial, and are often made with eggs, lemon juice and rice. Fasoláda is a popular thick bean soup; others include pepper soup (pipéri soúpa), with the addition of vegetables and meat, and clear bouillon (somós kreátos). There are also excellent fish soups (psárosoupes).

**Meat (kréas)**

The favourite kinds of meat are lamb (arnáki) and mutton (arní), usually roasted or grilled. Souvlákia and döner kebab (meat grilled on the spit) are also popular. Kokorétsi is lamb offal roasted on the spit.

**Vegetables and salads**

Typical vegetables are artichokes (angináres), aubergines (melitsánes), courgettes (kolokithákia) and peppers (pipériés), usually stuffed or cooked in oil. Salads include lettuce (maroúli), tomato salad (tomáto saláta), asparagus salad (sparángia saláta) and "country salad" (choriatikí), a mixture of lettuce, tomatoes, olives and ewe's-milk cheese.

**Fish (psári)**

Fish and seafood feature prominently on Greek menus. The commonest species are sea-bream (sinagrída, tsipoúra), sole (glóssa), red mullet (barboúni) and tunny (tónnos), together with lobsters (astakós), mussels (mídia), squid (kalamári) and octopus (oktapódi).

**Desserts (dessér)**

The commonest desserts are fruit or an ice (pagotó). There is a wide range of locally grown fruit, varying according to the season – melons (pepóni), water melons (karpoúzi), peaches (rodákino), pears (achládi), apples (mílo), oranges (portokáli), grapes (stafília) and figs (síka).

**Cheese (tirí)**

Greek cheeses are mostly made from ewes' or goats' milk, as is yoghurt (yaoúrti).

Other items which will appear on the table include bread (psomí), salt (aláti), pepper (pipéri) and sugar (záchari).

**Wine**

The commonest drink is wine (krasí), either red (mávro) or white (áspro). The ordinary table wines are resinated to improve their keeping qualities (retsína, krasí retsináto), and are characteristically sharp, which is an acquired taste. The better quality unresinated wines have been brought into line with EEC directives; they are identified by the letters VQPRD on the label.

**Beer (bíra)**

The brewing of beer in Greece dates from the reign of King Otto I, a native of Bavaria, and Greek beers, mostly brewed to Bavarian recipes, are excellent. The consumption of beer in Greece has increased considerably in recent years.

**Spirits (pnevmatódi potá)**

The commonest Greek aperitif is ouzo, an aniseed-flavoured spirit which can be diluted with water. Rakí is similar but stronger. Màsticha is a liqueur made from the bark of the mastic tree. Greek brandy (konyák) is fruity and fairly sweet.

These include water (neró), mineral water (metallikó neró, sóda), orangeade and lemonade (portokaláda, lemonáda) and freshly pressed fruit juices (portokaláda fréska, orange juice).

Coffee comes in different strengths and degrees of sweetness – e.g.: kafe glyko (very sweet), kafe metrio (medium sweet), kafe sketo (sugarless).

In addition to black tea (mávro tsai) there are various herb teas, such as tsai ménda (peppermint tea), kamoumíllo (camomile) and tsai tou vounoú (an infusion of mountain herbs).

The coffee-house (kafeníon) plays an important part in the life of the Greeks. It is not merely a place for drinking coffee, but has in a sense taken over the function of the ancient Greek agora as a place for meeting friends, for conversation, for playing cards and other games and for doing business.
Coffee is served with the accompaniment of a glass of water (neró). Ouzo, the national aperitif, is accompanied by various titbits – cheese, olives, etc. (meze).

There are also patisseries (zacharoplastío), which serve cakes and sweets as well as French coffee and other beverages. Greek sweets tend to be very sweet indeed.

## Galleries

Athens has a large number of art galleries which put on exhibitions of Greek and international art. The following is merely a selection.
Argo Gallery, Merlin 8
Art Arcade (Stoa Technis), Vourourestíou 45
Astor Gallery, Karageórgi Sérvias 16
Athens Art Hall, Glykonos 4 (Lykabettos)
Desmos Gallery, Sýngrou 4
Desmos Art Gallery, Akademías 28
Diogenes Gallery, Tsakalof 10
Diogenes Gallery, Nikis Street (Sýntagma)
Eggonopoulos Gallery, Kolonáki
Fine Art Centre, Zaimis 18
Iolas Zoumboulakis Gallery, Kolonáki 20
Kreonidis, Iperidou and Nikis
Medusa Gallery, Astydamantos 75
Ora Cultural Centre, Xenophontos 7
Rotonda Gallery, Skoufa 20
Tholos Gallery, Filellínon 20
Zoumboulakis Gallery, Kolonáki

## Getting to Athens

Motorists have a choice between the fairly strenuous journey through Yugoslavia, using the autoput (motorway), and the alternative route down through Italy and then by car ferry to Greece. There are a number of different ferry services:
Ancona–Piraeus (Libra Maritime), mid June to mid Oct., weekly

## Practical Information

Ancona–Piraeus (Med Sun Lines), weekly
Venice–Piraeus–Rhodes (Adriatica), weekly
Venice–Piraeus–Rhodes (Hellenic Mediterranean Lines), weekly

There are also a number of services from Ancona to Patras, 214 km (133 miles) W of Athens by motorway.

Information and reservations

Adriatica Line:
Sealink U.K. Ltd,
Victoria Station,
P.O. Box 29,
London SW1V 1JX;
tel. (01) 828 1940, 828 1948.

Hellenic Mediterranean Lines,
18 Hanover Street,
London W1R 9HG;
tel. (01) 499 0076.

Libra Maritime:
Lion International Travel Services Ltd,
71 Braeside Avenue,
Brighton BN1 8RN;
tel. (0273) 555403.

Med Sun Lines Ferry Ltd:
Cosmopolitan Holidays Ltd,
91 York Street,
London W1H 1DU;
tel. (01) 402 4255.

Documents, etc.

Driving licence, car registration document, international insurance certificate ("green card"), nationality plate, warning triangle.

By rail

The journey to Greece by rail is long, and may be made longer by delays. The best trains are the Athens Express (from Paris or Munich), the Acropolis Express (from Munich or Vienna) and the Hellas Express (from Cologne). Allowing for connections from London, the journey is likely to take approximately four days.

By bus

Euroways coaches (daily mid June to mid Oct., three times weekly the rest of the year) make the journey from London to Athens in $3\frac{1}{2}$ days, departing from Victoria Coach Station at 8 p.m. On the return journey the coach departs from the Peloponnese Station, Athens, at 8.30 a.m.
Information: Euroways Express Coaches Ltd, 8 Park Lane, Croydon CR9 1DN, tel. (01) 462 7733.
There is also a Europabus service (run by the Continental railways) from London to Athens, departing on Friday evenings from May to October.
Information: Sealink Travel Ltd, Inclusive Tours, Room 27, Eversholt House, 163–203 Eversholt Street, London NW1 1BG, tel. (01) 388 6846; or from main British Rail travel centres and stations.

By air

The quickest and easiest way to get to Athens is by air. There are daily scheduled services from London to Athens, as well as numerous charter flights, particularly during the holiday season.

# Hospitals (nosokomío)

First aid: dial 166 (24-hour service).

K.A.T. (Accident and Orthopaedic Hospital), Kifissiá Street, tel. (01) 8 01 44 41.

# Hotels (xenodochío)

Greek hotels are officially classified in six categories – L (luxury), A, B, C, D and E – and most visitors will look for accommodation in one of the first four categories.

Tariffs

The charge for a room may be increased by 10% for a stay of one or two days, and is likely to be some 20% higher between July and mid September than during the rest of the year.

The tariffs shown in the following table (in drachmas) are inclusive of service and taxes. Given the present trend of inflation, however, increases are to be expected.

|   | Single room | Double room |
|---|---|---|
| L | 610–1030 | 1060–1440 |
| A | 520–900 | 870–1250 |
| B | 520–900 | 870–1250 |
| C | 450–750 | 650–800 |
| D | 360–450 | 460–650 |
| E | 270–400 | 300–500 |

Athens and the immediately surrounding area are well provided with hotels, most of them of fairly recent construction. Advance reservation is, however, advisable, particularly during the main holiday seasons (Easter, June–September).

Reservations

Information and reservations: Greek Hotel Chamber, 6 Aristídou Street, tel. 3 23 66 41.

Bookings can also be made through the hotel reservation desk of the Greek National Tourist Organisation, 2 Karageórgi Sérvias Street (Sýntagma Square), tel. 3 23 71 93, which is open Mon.–Sat. 8.30 a.m.–2 p.m. and 2.30–5.30 p.m., Sun. 10 a.m.–3 p.m.

Amalia, Leofóros Amalías 10, L, 188 beds
Athénée Palace, Kolokotrónia 1, L, 176 b.
Athens Hilton, Leofóros Vas. Sofías, L, 960 b.
Caravel, Leofóros Vas. Alexándrou 2, L, 841 b.
Grande Bretagne, Sýntagma Square, L, 662 b.
King George, Sýntagma Square, L, 223 b.
King's Palace, Panepistimíou 4, L, 396 b.
St George Lycabettus, Dexaméni Square, L, 278 b.
Astor, Karageórgi Sérvias 16, A, 234 b.
Attika Palace, Karageórgi Sérvias 6, A, 147 b.
Electra, Ermoú 5, A, 180 b.
Electra Palace, Nikodímou 18, A, 196 b.
Esperia, Stadíou 22, A, 338 b.
Olympic Palace, Filellínon 16, A, 168 b.
Adrian, Adrianoú 74, B, 44 b.
Arethusa, Mitropóleos 6–8, B, 158 b.
Athens Gate, Leofóros Sýngrou 10, B, 202 b.
Athinais, Leofóros Vas. Sofías 99, B, 162 b.
Christina, Kalliróis 15, B, 173 b.
Galaxy, Akadimías 22, B, 192 b.
Metropol, Stadíou 55, B, 100 b.

Around Sýntagma Square

# Practical Information

Minerva, Stadíou 3, B, 86 b.
Omiros, Apóllonos 15, B, 60 b.
Palladion, Panepistimíou 54, B, 115 b.
Pan, Mitropóleos 11, B, 92 b.
Plaka, Kapnikaréas 7, B, 123 b.
Titania, Panepistimíou 52–54, B, 754 b.
Aphrodite, Apóllonos 21, C, 162 b.
Carolina, Kolokotróni 55, C, 57 b.
Caryatis, Nikodímou 31, C, 50 b.
Hermes, Apóllonos 19, C, 85 b.

Around Omónia Square

Ambassadeurs, Sokrátous 67, A, 370 b.
King Minos, Pireós 1, A, 287 b.
Academos, Akadimías 58, B, 220 b.
Achillion, Ayíou Konstantínou 32, B, 980 b.
Alfa, Chalkokondýli 17, B, 167 b.
Arcadia, Márni 46, B, 154 b.
Athens Center, Sofokléous 26, B, 259 b.
Cairo City, Márni 42, B, 140 b.
Candia, Deliyánni 40, B, 252 b.
Delphi, Platía Ayíou Konstantínou 1, B, 93 b.
Dorian Inn, Pireós 15–19, B, 287 b.
El Greco, Athinás 65, B, 167 b.
Eretria, Chalkokondýli 12, B, 119 b.
Grand Hotel, Veranzérou 10, B, 190 b.
Ilion, Ayíou Konstantínou 7, B, 166 b.
Ionis, Chalkokondy1li 41, B, 194 b.
Marathon, Karólou 23, B, 174 b.
Marmara, Chalkokondýli 14, B, 252 b.
Minoa, Karólou 12, B, 80 b.
Alcestis, Platía Theátrou 18, C, 224 b.
Amaryllis, Veranzérou 45, C, 98 b.
Ares, Pireós 7, C, 71 b.
Arias, Karólou 20, C, 89 b.
Aristides, Sokrátous 50, C, 158 b.
Artemis, Veranzérou 20, C, 79 b.
Aspasia, Satovriándou 26, C, 65 b.
Astra, Deliyánni 46, C, 48 b.
Asty, Pireós 2, C, 224 b.
Atlas, Sofokléous 30, C, 33 b.
Attalos, Athinás 29, C, 155 b.
Banghion, Omónia 18B, C, 93 b.
Capitol, Omónia, C, 168 b.
Carlton, Omónia 7, C, 60 b.
Diros, Ayíou Konstantínou 21, C, 84 b.
Elite, Pireós 23, C, 80 b.
Europa, Satovriándou 7, C, 67 b.
Euripides, Evripídou 79, C, 119 b.
Mediterranean, Veranzérou 28, C, 82 b.
Nausikaa, Karólou 21, C, 73 b.
Nestor, Ayíou Konstantínou 58, C, 95 b.
Odeon, Pireós 42, C, 98 b.
Olympia, Pireós 25, C, 74 b.
Orpheus, Chalkokondýli 58, C, 71 b.
Oscar, Samoú 25, C, 151 b.

Near National Museum

Acropole Palace, 28 Oktovríou 51, L, 173 b.
Park, Leofóros Alexándras 10, L, 279 b.
Divani-Zafolia, Leofóros Alexándras 87–89, A, 353 b.
Atlantic, Solomoú 60, B, 275 b.
Plaza, Acharnón 78, B, 239 b.
Xenophon, Acharnón 340, B, 310 b.
Aristoteles, Acharnón 15, C, 102 b.

Morpheus, Aristotélous 3, C, 35 b.
Museum, Bubulínas and Tósitsa, C, 108 b.
Paradise Rock, Acharnón 50, C, 97 b.

Anagenisis, C, 18 b.                                              Amaroússion

Pentelikon, Deliyánni 66, L, 112 b.                               Kifissià
Apergi, Deliyánni 59, A, 183 b.
Attikon, Pentélis 12, A, 41 b.
Cecil, Xenías 7, A, 150 b.
Cóstis Dimitradópoulos, Deliyánni, A, 54 b.
Grand Chalet, Kokkinára 38, A, 38 b.
Palace, Kolokotróni 1, A, 150 b.
Semiramis, Chariláou Trikoúpi 36, A, 78 b.
Theoxenia, Filádelfos 2, A, 120 b.
Nausikaa, Péllis 6, B, 30 b.
And several hotels in categories C, D and E.

Casino Mont Parnes, L, 212 b. (alt. 1050 m – 3445 ft)            Párnis
Xenia, B. 300 b.

Achillion, Pálea Pentéli, C, 21 b.                                Pentélikor

---

# Information

---

National Tourist Organisation of Greece,                          United Kingdom
195–197 Regent Street, London W1R 8DR, tel. (01) 734
5997.

Olympic Tower, 645 Fifth Avenue, New York, NY 10022, tel.        United States
(212) 421 5777.
627 West Sixth Street, Los Angeles, CA 90017, tel. (213) 626
6696.
168 North Michigan Avenue, Chicago, IL 60601, tel. (312)
782 1084.

National Tourist Organisation of Greece,                          Canada
Suite 67, 2 Place Ville Marie, Esso Plaza, Montreal, Quebec
H3B 2C9, tel. (514) 871 1535.

National Tourist Organisation of Greece,                          In Athens
Karageórgi Sérvias 2, tel. 3 22 25 45.
Open 8.45 a.m.–8 p.m.

Also Amerikis S. 2, near Sýntagma Square (Head Office),
tel. 3 22 31 11.

Stoa Spiroumilíous, tel. 3 22 14 59.
Open 8 a.m.–2 p.m. and 5–8 p.m.
Sale of Festival tickets.

Ellinikó Airport, tel. 9 79 95 00.
Open 9 a.m.–8 p.m.

Information can also be obtained from the Tourist Police in        Tourist Police
Athens (Sýngrou 7) and elsewhere. In the Athens area dial
01/171.

Railway Travel Service (OSE), Karólou 1–3, tel. 5 22 24 91.       Rail services
At Larissa Station, tel. 8 21 38 82 and 8 23 32 35.
At Peloponnese Station, tel. 5 13 16 87.

## Practical Information

Boat services

Aegean: Harbour Office, Piraeus, tel. 4 61 13 11.
Saronic Gulf: Harbour Office, Piraeus, tel. 4 61 13 11.
Fast boats in Saronic Gulf: tel. 4 53 14 16 and 4 52 12 72.

Air services

Olympic Airways, tel. 9 81 12 01.

# Language

The national language is modern Greek. In towns and tourist areas English is widely understood.
The following is the Greek alphabet:

| Letter | | Anc. Gk | Mod. Gk | Pronunciation |
|---|---|---|---|---|
| A | α | alpha | álfa | a, semi-long, as in "apple" |
| B | β | beta | víta | v |
| Γ | γ | gamma | gháma | gh; y before e or i |
| Δ | δ | delta | dhélta | dh as in "the" |
| E | ε | epsilon | épsilon | e, open, semi-long, as in "egg" |
| Z | ζ | zeta | zíta | z |
| H | η | eta | íta | ee, semi-long, as in "cheese" |
| Θ | θ | theta | thíta | th as in "thin" |
| I | ι | iota | ióta | i, semi-long, as in "cheese" |
| K | κ | kappa | kápa | k, ky |
| Λ | λ | lambda | lámdha | l |
| M | μ | mu | mi | m |
| N | ν | nu | ni | n |
| Ξ | ξ | xi | ksi | ks |
| O | o | omicron | ómikron | o, open, semi-long |
| Π | π | pi | pi | p |
| P | ρ | rho | ro | r, lightly rolled |
| Σ | σ[1] | sigma | síghma | s |
| T | τ | tau | taf | t |
| Y | υ | ypsilon | ípsilon | i, as in "egg" |
| Φ | φ | phi | fi | f |
| X | χ | chi | khi | ch as in Scottish "loch"; before e or i, somewhere between ch and sh |
| Ψ | ψ | psi | psi | ps |
| Ω | ω | omega | omégha | o, open, semi-long |

[1] written ς at the end of a word

# Lost property office (grafío evréseos apolesténdon)

The main lost property office is at 14 Messógion Street, tel. 7 70 57 11.

For objects lost on taxis and buses the number to ring is 5 23 01 11.

# Motoring

Road signs and traffic regulations are in line with international standards. Traffic travels on the right, with overtaking on the left.
The use of the horn is prohibited in built-up areas.
It is an offence to drive after drinking *any* alcohol.
In brightly lit built-up areas only sidelights are normally used. Some drivers switch their lights off altogether when meeting another car.
The speed limit for passenger vehicles is 50 km/p.h. (31 m.p.h.) in built-up areas, 80 km/p.h. (50 m.p.h.) on ordinary roads and 100 km/p.h. (62 m.p.h.) on motorways and expressways.

E.L.P.A. (Automobile and Touring Ciub of Greece), 2–4 Messógion Street, tel. (01) 7 79 16 15–19.
Information about road conditions, etc.

Greek Touring Club, 12 Polytechníou Street, tel. (01) 5 24 86 01.

Information

E.L.P.A.: dial 114.
The breakdown service operates over a radius of 60 km (37 miles) from Athens. The charge for answering a call is 300 dr.; a towing charge of 20 dr. per kilometre is made to non-members. Free to foreign motorists.
The main tourist routes are patrolled from April to September by the yellow vehicles of the E.L.P.A. breakdown service, marked "Assistance Routière". Drivers in need of assistance should indicate this by raising the bonnet of their car or waving a yellow cloth.

Breakdown service

BMW: Vas. Georgíou and Ikarías 6, tel. 5 71 13 90.
Fiat: Ayías Annis 7, Votanikós, tel. 3 46 62 33.
Ford: Piapouta 10, Argyroúpolis, tel. 9 22 99 00–02.
Mercedes: Athinón 40, tel. 5 71 19 01.
Opel: Sýngrou 340, tel. 9422 43 21.
Renault: Lenorman and Kifíssou, Terma Kolokýnthous, tel. 5 12 81 05 and 5 12 88 17.
Simca: Vouliagménis, tel. 99 27 10–13.
Volkswagen, NSU, Audi: Acharnón and Milliaráki, tel. 2 02 45 70–72; Vouliagménis, tel. 9 92 28 11–13.

Service garages

# Museums

Acropolis Museum
See A to Z

Agora Museum
See A to Z

Benáki Museum
See A to Z

## Practical Information

Byzantime Museum
See A to Z

Ceramics, Museum of,
Monastiráki Square.
Buses: 10, 72
Open 10 a.m.–2 p.m.; closed Tues.

Folk Art, Museum of,
17 Kydathinéon Street (Pláka).
Trolleybuses: 1, 2, 5, 12
Open 9.30 a.m.–1.30 p.m.; closed Mon.

Kanellópoulos Museum
See A to Z

Kerameikos Museum
See A to Z, Kerameikos Cemetery

King Otto Museum
See A to Z

Marathon Museum
See A to Z, Marathon

Military Museum
See A to Z

National Archaeological Museum
See A to Z

National Gallery
See A to Z

National Historical Museum
See A to Z, Old Parliament

# Music

Concert halls

Parnassos Hall,
Georgiou Karytsi 8, tel. 3 23 87 45.
This hall, near Sýntagma Square, is the oldest concert hall in
Athens and was built in the 19th c. Concerts are frequently
given here by students of the Athens Conservatoire (admission
free).
Most concerts take place in the foreign cultural institutes
(Institut Français, Goethe-Institut, Instituto Italiano, etc.).

Programme

See Events

# Newspapers (efimerída, periodikó)

British newspapers are available at street kiosks in central
Athens late on the day of publication.
There are two local English-language papers, the "Athens
Daily News" and "Athens Daily Post".

# Night life

Angela
Glyfáda Square.
Open daily 8 p.m.–2 a.m.

Atheneum
Michalakopoúlou 39.

Apollo
Lisíou 15 (Pláka).
Open daily 8 p.m.–2.30 a.m., Sat. 8 p.m.–4 a.m., Sun. 7
p.m.–2.30 a.m.

Athens Hilton Galaxy Bar
Papadiamantopoúlou 4.
Open daily 10 p.m.–3 a.m.

Camping
Néa Kifissiá.
Open daily 9.30 p.m.–2 a.m.

Kariatis
Flessa 11.
Open daily 8 p.m.–2.30 a.m., Sun. 7 p.m.–2.30 a.m.

Nine Muses
Akadimías 43.
One of the best Athenian discos.

Olympic Venus
Glikerias Galatsi 7.
Open 9 p.m.–2 a.m.

Stardust
Vas. Alexándrou 5–7 (behind the Hilton).

Athenaia, Posidónos 63
Aigokeros, Lisíou 15 (Pláka)

With bouzouki music

Napoleon, Lisíou 20 (Pláka)
Panorama, Acharnón 77
Sirene, Posidónos
Zorbas, Amerikís 6
Kantari, Diochárous 3 (behind the Hilton)
Konaki, Diochárous 11 (behind the Hilton)
Nostalgia, Kalimnou 11
O Imeros tou Aria, Chelidónous Kómbos, Néa Kifissiá
Neraida, Vas. Georgíou Kalamáki 2
Nuit d'Athènes, Patissión and Agathoupóleos 12
Storck, Ayios Kosmás

Night-clubs

Coronet
Panepistimíou 6.
Open daily from 10 p.m.

Striptease

Maxim
Othonos 6 (Sýntagma Square).
Open daily from 11 p.m.

## Opening times

| | |
|---|---|
| Bánks | Banks are open Mon.–Fri. 9 a.m.–1.30 p.m.<br>The Bank of Greece branch at Ellinikón airport is open day and night. |
| Chemists | Chemists' opening times vary over the year. They are normally as follows:<br>Summer: Mon.–Sat. 8.30 a.m.–1.30 p.m. (2.30 p.m.); Tues., Thurs. and Fri. 5.30–8.30 p.m.<br>Winter: Mon.–Sat. 8.30 a.m.–1.30 p.m.; Tues., Thurs. and Fri. 4.30–7.30 p.m. |
| Hairdressers | Summer: Mon. and Wed. 8 a.m.–2 p.m., Tues., Thurs. and Fri. 8 a.m.–1.30 p.m. and 5–9 p.m., Sat. 8 a.m.–4 p.m.<br>Winter: Mon. and Wed. 8.15 a.m.–2 p.m., Tues., Thurs. and Fri. 8.15 a.m.–1.30 p.m. and 4.30–8.30 p.m., Sat. 8.15 a.m.–5 p.m. |
| Museums | Opening times are shown in the entries for the various museums in the "A to Z" section. |
| Post offices | See under Post offices below. |
| Shops | Opening times vary from shop to shop. The following times are no more than a broad average:<br>May–Oct.: Mon., Wed. and Sat. 8.30 a.m.–2.30 p.m.; Tues., Thurs. and Fri. 8.30 a.m.–1.30 p.m. and 5.30–8.30 p.m.<br>Oct.–May: Mon., Wed. and Sat. 8.30 a.m.–2.30 p.m.; Tues., Thurs. and Fri. 8.30 a.m.–1.30 p.m. and 5–8 p.m. |
| Souvenir shops | Mon.–Sat. 8.30 a.m.–9.30 p.m., Sun. 9 a.m.–3 p.m. |

## Pets

Dogs and cats are admitted to Greece only on production of a veterinary certificate of health and, in the case of dogs, a certificate that they have been inoculated against rabies not more than a year before entry.

Because of their own quarantine regulations, however, it is unlikely that British and other English-speaking visitors will want to take their pets to Greece.

## Photography

Photography and cine-photography are permitted in museums and on archaeological sites without any other formality than the purchase of an additional ticket, provided that neither flash nor a tripod is used. Photographers who want to use a tripod must obtain a special permit from the Ministry of Culture, 14 Aristídou Street (office hours Mon., Wed. and Fri. 11 a.m.–1 p.m.).

The photographing of military installations is prohibited.

## Police (astimonía)

To call the police in Athens dial 100, in the suburbs 109. The best plan for visitors is to apply in the first place to the tourist police (dial 171).
For other emergency telephone numbers see the last page.

## Post offices (tachidromía)

Eólou Street 100.
Open daily 7.30 a.m.–7.30 p.m., Sun. 9 a.m.–1 p.m.
Corner of Mitropóleos Street and Sýntagma Square.
Open daily 7 a.m.–10 p.m., Sun. 9 a.m.–8 p.m.

Head post offices

Mon.–Sat. 7.30 a.m.–7.30 p.m.

Opening times

Parcels weighing over 1 kg (2 lb 3 oz) are accepted only at the following post offices:
Koumountoúrou 29 (near the National Theatre)
Psychikó
Stadíou 4 (in the arcades)
Ampelokipi

Parcel post

Parcels and registered letters must be presented open for inspection.

Letters within Greece cost 8 dr. (up to 20 g); to Western Europe by air mail 17 dr. (20 g); to the USA and Canada by air 18 dr. (10 g) or 22 dr. (20 g).

Postal tariffs

Postcards cost 6 dr. within Greece, 10 dr. to western Europe and 12 dr. to the USA and Canada (all by surface mail).

## Public holidays and feast days

The following days are statutory public holidays:
New Year's Day (1 January), Epiphany (6 January), Independence Day (25 March), Ochi Day (28 October: "No" Day, commemorating the Greek rejection of the Italian ultimatum in 1940), Christmas Day (25 December).

Statutory public holidays

In addition to the statutory holidays there are a series of religious festivals, the most important of which are the following:
Easter (with a service which lasts through the night into the early hours of Easter Day);
Whitsun;
the Annunciation; and
the Dormition (Assumption).
On these days shops are closed.

Religious feast days

# Radio

There are news bulletins in English, French and German daily at
7.15 a.m.

# Railway stations (stathmi)

Main (Larissa) Station

The Larissa Station (Státhmos Laríssis) is the terminus of the
State Railways lines to Piraeus and to Salonica and
Alexandroúpolis.

Peloponnese Station

The Peloponnese Station is the main station of the narrow-
gauge Peloponnese Railway (SPAP: trains from Piraeus to
Corinth, Patras, Trípolis and Kalamáta).

# Restaurants

Lunch is served from noon to 3 p.m., dinner from 8 to 11 p.m.
The restaurants of the higher categories offer international
cuisine, the tavernas and smaller restaurants Greek food. In
most restaurants and tavernas it is the practice to go into the
kitchen and choose your meal there. In the larger establishments the menu will be written in English or some other
western language as well as in Greek.

Luxury restaurants

Athens Hilton Supper Club
Hilton Hotel, tel. 72 02 01.
Closed Mon.
International menu.

Blue Pine
Tsaldári 27, Kifissiá, tel. 8 01 29 69.
Open daily 8.30 p.m.–1 a.m.; closed Sun.
Very expensive; numerous special meat dishes.

Grande Bretagne
Sýntagma Square, tel. 3 23 02 51.
In the oldest and best known hotel in Athens.
Meals served at same time as for hotel guests (1–3 p.m. and
8–10.30 p.m.).

Riva
Michalakopoulou 114, tel. 7 70 66 11.
Open 7.30 p.m.–1 a.m.; closed Sun.
French cuisine.

Dionissos
Dionisíou Areopagítou Street (facing Acropolis), tel. 9 23 19
26, 9 23 31 82.
Open 1–4 p.m., 7 p.m.–1 a.m.
A very expensive restaurant with a fantastic view of the
Parthenon.

Al Tartufo
Posidónos 65, Paleón Fáliron, tel. 9 82 65 60.
Open daily from 7.30 p.m.
Italian cuisine.

International cuisine

Bagatelle
K. Ventíri 9 (near Hilton Hotel), tel. 73 03 49.
Open at lunch-time until 3.30 p.m. and 7 p.m.–1 a.m.; closed
Sun.
French cuisine.

Erato
Varnali 7, Chalándri.
French cuisine, reasonably priced.

Hickory Grill
Niréos and Posidónos, Paleón Fáliron, tel. 9 82 19 72.
Open daily 7.30 p.m.–1 a.m.

Kyoto
Garibaldi 5 (on Hill of the Muses), tel. 9 23 20 47.
Closed Sun.
Japanese cuisine.

Le Calvados
Alkános 3, tel. 8 94 26 05.
Open daily 8 p.m.–2 a.m.; closed Sun.

Pagoda
Bousgou 2, tel. 3 60 24 66.
Open daily 1–3 p.m. and 7 p.m.–1 a.m.
Chinese cuisine, with Cantonese specialties.

Papaki
Iránou 5, tel. 71 24 21.
Open daily from 8 p.m.
Greek and French cuisine (duck a specialty).

Ritterburg
Formiónos 11, Pangráti, tel. 73 84 21.
Open daily 1–4 p.m. and 7.30 p.m.–1.30 a.m.
German cuisine.

Corfu
Kriezótou 6, tel. 3 61 30 11.
Open midday–midnight.

Greek cuisine

✳ Gerofinikas
Pindárou 10, tel. 3 62 27 19.
Open daily 12.20 p.m.–midnight.

Nefeli
Pános 24, tel. 3 21 24 75.
Reservation necessary on Sat. and Sun.

Ponderossa
Amalías 8, Kifissiá, tel. 8 01 23 56.
Open daily from 9 p.m.; closed Sun. and school holidays.

*Taverna with music: a popular tourist attraction*

Psaropoulos
Kalamoú 2, Glyfáda, tel. 8 94 56 77.
Open daily noon–3.30 p.m. and 8 p.m.–midnight.
Fish a specialty.

Vassilis
Voukourestíou 14A, tel. 3 61 28 01.

Tavernas

Reasonably priced restaurants in an unpretentious setting.
Mainly Greek dishes.

Askimopapo, Iónon 61, Ano Petralóna
Kavalieratos, Tatoiou 82, Metamórfosis
Leonidas, corner Eólou 12 and Iasonos 5
O Nikas, Skopelou 5, Kifissiá
Rodia, Aristippou 44, Kolonáki
To Katsiki, Athinaion 12, Galatsi
To Limanaki, at end of Avras, between Kavouri and Vouliagméni

Tavernas with music

Asterias, Folegandrou 41
Belle Maison, Fokeas 6, Platía Viktorias
Hatzakos, Irodou Attikou 41, Maroússi
Lito, Flessa and Tripódon, Pláka
Myrtia, Markou Mousouri 35
Psatha, Ioannou Drosópoulou 110
To Tzaki, Vas. Konṣtantínou 12, Glyfáda
● Xynou, Angelou Yerondos 4, Pláka, tel. 3 22 10 65 (reservation necessary)

*Craftsmen's shops in an old Athens street*

## Shopping

Athens has a great variety of shops to tempt the visitor. They are particularly numerous in the following areas:

In this area there are many luxury shops, selling men's, women's and children's clothing, leather articles, furs, jewellery, gifts, antiques, books, records, folk art, etc.

Sýntagma Square and Kolonáki Square

Here too can be found a great range of tempting goods, with a rather lower price level.

Omónia Square

Athinás Street runs through the middle of the market quarter, with the various kinds of shops concentrated in particular streets. Here can be found clothing, shoes and household requisites as well as foodstuffs. The area round Monastiráki Square has many shops selling copperware, handicrafts, antiques, furniture, etc. On Sunday mornings a flea-market is held here.

Athinás Street and Monastiráki Square

Here, too, are shops of all kinds, including furniture and clothing.

Patissia Street and Kýpseli quarter

This port town is also a busy commercial town, offering a wide range of wares at prices which are usually lower than in Athens.

Piraeus

National Organisation of Greek Handicrafts, Mitropóleos 9 (display only). Handicraft articles can be bought at the following showrooms:
Ethnikí Prónia, Ipatías 6; branches at Vourourestíou 24 and Hilton Hotel

Folk arts and crafts

153

Ikotechnia of the Greek Lyceum, Dimokrítou 17
Ergastírion Aporon Gynekón, Voukourestíou 13
World Craft Council (Hellenic Section), 135 Vass. Sofias Ave,
Athens

## Sightseeing tours

On foot

Sightseeing walks are conducted by properly trained local guides.
Information: Association of Greek Guides, Apóllonos 9A, tel. 3 22 97 05.

By bus

The following coach trips are run:
Half-day.
City tour, with visit to Archaeological Museum or Benáki Museum and Acropolis.
Daily, 9 a.m.–1 p.m.

Afternoon tour of Athens.
1 April–15 Sept., 3.30–6.30 p.m.; 16 Sept.–31 March, 3–6 p.m.

Athens by night.
Daily, 8.30 p.m.–12.30 a.m.

To Soúnion.
1 April–15 Sept., 3.30–7.30 p.m.; 16 Sept.–31 March, 3–7 p.m.

Whole-day.
Athens–Corinth–Mycenae–Argos–Nauplia–Epidauros–Athens.
Daily, 8.30 a.m.–7 p.m.

Athens–Thebes–Levadia–Arachova–Delphi–Athens.
Daily, 8.15 a.m.–7 p.m.

Information about other sightseeing trips and excursions can be obtained from travel agencies (see below) and from most hotels.

From the air

An unusual way of sightseeing is to charter a light aircraft and get a bird's-eye view of Athens and the surrounding area. The official charter agency is Olympic Aviation, at the West Terminal, Ellinikón Airport, tel. 9 81 12 11. The pilot is also supplied by the agency.

Visitors with a pilot's licence can apply to:
National Aeroclub, Akadimías 27A, tel. 3 61 62 05.
Piraeus Aeroclub, Vas. Sofías Street, Piraeus, tel. 4 11 01 20.

## Souvenirs

Traditional handicrafts, often of very high quality (copperware, brassware, etc.), are mainly to be found in the area around Monastiráki Square and Pandrósou Street.

# Sport

Athens and the surrounding area offer a wide range of facilities for sport.

Glyfáda, tel. 8 94 68 20.                                          Golf
A first-class course (18 holes) 12 km (7½ miles) from Athens.

Greek Riding Club, Amaroússi, Paradísou 18, tel. 6 81 25 06.      Riding
Athens Riding Club, Géraka, Ayía Paraskeví, tel. 6 59 38 03.
Tatoi Riding Club, Varimbóbi, tel. 8 08 18 44.
Attic Riding Club, Polidéndri, Kapandríti, tel. 0 29 5 – 5 20 78;
30 km (19 miles) N of Athens on the national highway.
Varimbóbi Riding Club, Varimbóbi, tel. 8 01 99 12.
All riding clubs are open to non-members.

Information from the Greek Rowing Association, 34             Rowing
Voukourestíou Street, Athens, tel. 3 61 21 09.

Information from the Greek Sailing Association, 15A          Sailing
Xenofóntos Street, Athens, tel. 3 23 68 13.
A sailing school is run by the Paleó Fáliro Naval Club,
tel. 9 81 58 35.

Bathing beaches on the "Apollo Coast" and on the E coast of    Swimming
Attica.

There are tennis courts at the bathing stations of the National   Tennis
Tourist Organisation of Greece:
Alipedou Voúlas A Beach, tel. 8 95 32 8.
Alipedou Voúlas B Beach, tel. 8 95 95 69 and 8 59 95 90.
Vouliagméni, tel. 8 96 09 06.
Várkitsa, tel. 8 97 21 02.

There are also courts at the following sports centres:
Ayios Kosmás, tel. 9 81 21 12.
Athens Tennis Club, Leofóros Vas. Olgas 2, tel. 9 23 28 72.
Attic Tennis Club, Filothéi, tel. 6 81 25 57.
Kifissiá Athletic Club, 45 Tatoi Street, tel. 8 01 31 00.
Néa Smýrni Athletic Club, tel. 9 33 12 28.
Panhellenic Gymnastic Club, 26 Mavromatéon Street,
tel. 8 23 37 20.
Glyfáda Naval and Athletic Club, tel. 8 94 65 79.

There are water-skiing schools at Kavoúri, Lagonísi, Várkitsa   Water-skiing
and Vouliagméni.

# Taxis

Athens taxis have meters. The hire charge is 15 dr., plus 13.50    Fares
dr. per kilometre within the Athens–Piraeus city area
(extending to Ekáli, Pérama, Eleusis, Várkitsa and Ayía
Paraskeví), but these prices are expected to rise.

Ayía Paraskeví, tel. 6 59 24 44.                              Taxi ranks
Ayía Paraskeví–Stavrós, tel. 6 59 43 45.

Amaroússion, tel. 8 02 08 18.
Glyfáda, tel. 8 94 45 31.
Chalándri, tel. 6 81 27 81.
Kalamáki, tel. 9 81 81 03.
Kifissiá Square, tel. 8 01 22 70.
Sýntagma Square, tel. 3 23 79 42.

## Telegrams

To send a telegram dial 165 (abroad), 155 (within Greece).

The Athens telegraph and telephone office is at 15 Stadíou Street.

## Telephone (tiléfono)

International telephone dialling codes:
from the United Kingdom to Greece
010 30 (Athens 010 30 1)

from the United States or Canada to Greece
011 30 (Athens 011 30 1)

from Greece to the United Kingdom
00 44

from Greece to the United States or Canada
00 1

Directory enquiries, Athens: dial 131.
Directory enquiries, rest of Greece: 132.
General information on Greek telephone system: 134.
Speaking clock: 141.

A 3-minute call to the United Kingdom costs 102 dr., to the United States (New York) or Canada 270 dr.

## Theatre (téatro)

Athina, Derigny 10, tel. 8 23 73 30.
Diana, Hippokrátous 7, tel. 3 62 69 56.
National Opera (Olympia Theatre), Akadimías 59, tel. 3 61 24 61.
National Theatre, Ayíou Konstantínou (Omónia Square), tel. 3 22 14 59.
Superstar, Ayíou Meletíou and Patissión, tel. 8 64 07 74.
Vergi, Voukourestíou 1, tel. 3 23 52 35.

Open-air performances

Deflinario, Fáliron (on the Piraeus road).
Odeion of Herodes Atticus (see Events).

*Son et lumière*

From April to October a *son et lumière* show is presented on the Pynx, with illumination of the Acropolis and commentaries (in

English at certain performances) bringing out the highlights of
the Greek Classical period. Tickets at the entrance or by
telephoning 3 22 14 59 or 9 22 62 10.

## Time

Greece is on East European Time, 2 hours ahead of Greenwich
Mean Time.

## Tipping

Hotel tariffs normally include a service charge; where they do
not, 15% is appropriate (as in restaurants as well). In
restaurants it is usual to round up the payment to the waiter
(garsón) and in addition to leave some small amount for the
boy who assists him (mikrós).

In taxis it is usual to round up the amount paid to the driver.

## Transport

There are numerous bus and trolleybus services within
Athens, as well as country buses to places in Attica and other
parts of Greece.

| | |
|---|---|
| Platía Attikís–Larissa Station–Omónia–Sýntagma–Makriyánni–Veíkou–Kallithéa<br>Kýpseli–Stadíou–Filellínon–Profítis Ilías<br>Patissiá–Akadimías–Ampelokípi<br>Patissiá–Omónia–Sýntagma–Makriyánni–Koukáki | Trolleybuses (yellow) |
| No. 70 from Omónia<br>No. 165 from Filellínon | Green buses, Athens–Piraeus |
| From Mavromatéon to Grammatikó, Marathón, Máti, Néa Mákri, Rafína and Soúli<br>From Platía Egýptou to Afidna, Ayii Apóstoli, Amfiárion, Anávyssos, Káto Soúli, Keratéa, Lagoníssi, Lávrion, Legrená, Markópoulo, Oropós, Pórto Ráfti and Soúnion<br>From Vasiléos Iraklíou (National Museum): 105 to Paleá Pendéli, 106 to Néa Pendéli<br>From Stournári: 21 to Maroússi. From the nearby Platía Ayíou Konstantínou: 61 to Kolónos<br>From Alkiviádou: 64 to Filí, 116 to Párnis<br>From Koumoundoúrou: 98 to Ayía Varvára, 62 to Akadimías Plátonos, 67 to Asprópyrgos, 68 to Elefsina (Eleusis)<br>From Kaníngou: 132 to Ayios Stéfanos, 23 to Drossiá, 133 to Dionysós, 22 to Ekáli, X to Chalándri, 39/52 to Kaisarianí, 18 to Kifissiá, 134 to Krionéri, 50 to Lykabettos and Máraslion, 137 to Lake Marathón, 19 to Maroússi, 138 to Varybóbi<br>From Akademías (behind the University): 167 to Ayía Paraskeví, 42 to Psychikó, 41 to Anó Liossía | Blue city buses and buses to Attica |

## Practical Information

From Sýntagma (Othonos): 1A to Ayios Kosmás and West Airport
From Amalías: East Airport (direct)
From Amalías: 184 to East Airport
From Leofóros Olgas: 89 to Vouliagméni, 98 to Várkitsa
From Thíssion: 96 to Loútsa, 46 to Korópi, 42 to Palíni, 44 to Peanía, 45 to Spáta
From Asomáton: Ayii Theódori, Erétria, Mégara, Pórto Germenó, Vília
From Platía Eleftherías: 68 to Eleusis, 88 to Pérama, 100/67 to Dafní and Asprópyrgos

Country buses

To the western Peloponnese and western and northern Greece: departures from Kifissoú (reached on bus 62).
To Euboea and eastern and central Greece: departures from Liossíon 260 (reached on bus 63/64 or 113/114).

Electric Railway

The Electric Railway (Ilektrikós) runs from the northern suburb of Kifissiá through Athens to Piraeus, running underground for part of the way. The stations within the Athens city area, from N to S, are Attiki, Victoria, Omónia, Monastiráki and Thíssion.

Information

For information on all bus services dial 142.

## Travel agencies (grafía taxidión)

Hermès en Grèce, Stadíou 4, tel. 3 23 74 31. 3 22 73 42.
Horizon, Nikis 14, tel. 3 23 31 44.
Iberia Mericanos, Voukourestíou 18, tel. 3 63 92 00.
Kosmos, Mitropóleos 1, tel. 3 22 08 73.
Ley's Tours, Venizeloú 15, tel. 3 22 18 60.
Orion, Ayíou Konstantínou 5, tel. 5 22 44 07.
Pacific, Nikis 26, tel. 3 22 32 13.
Trans Mour, Stadíou 3, tel. 3 23 47 77.
Viking, Filellínon 3, tel. 3 22 93 87.
Wagons-Lits Cook, Karagéorgi Sérvias 2, tel. 3 24 22 81.

## Travel documents

Visitors from the United Kingdom, Commonwealth countries and the United States require only a valid passport for a stay of not more than 3 months. If they wish to stay longer than 3 months they must apply for an extension, at least 20 days before the end of the period, to the Aliens Police (Astinomía Allodapón, Chalkokondýli 9).

British driving licences and registration documents are accepted in Greece. Drivers from most other countries must have an international driving licence.

An international insurance certificate ("green card") valid for Greece is required.

Cars must bear an oval nationality plate.

# Youth hostels (xenones neoléas)

Hostel 1, Kypselis 57 and Ayíou Meletíou, tel. 8 22 58 60–63.
Trolleybus 2.
Hostel 2, Kallipóleos 20, Výrona, tel. 7 66 48 89. Bus 103 to
Tziràkopoúlou.
YMCA, Omírou 28 and Akadimías, tel. 3 62 69 70.
YWCA, Amerikís 11, tel. 3 62 42 91.

Information: Organosis Xenonon Neotitos Ellados (Greek
Youth Hostel Association), Dragatsaníou 4, Platía Klafthmónos, tel. 3 23 41 07 and 3 23 75 90.

## Useful Telephone Numbers at a Glance

Emergency calls
Police — 100
Tourist Police — 171
First Aid — 166
Red Cross (ambulance) — 150
Fire service — 199
ELPA breakdown service — 114
Chemists — 107
Dental emergency service (at night) — 6 43 00 01

Tourist information
NTOG main office — 3 22 25 45
Stoa Spiromilíous — 3 22 14 59
Ellinikón Airport — 9 79 95 00
Conducted tours — 3 22 97 05

Information on rail services — 145, 147
Information on bus services — 142

Airlines
Olympic Airways — 92 92/1
Flight information — 9 81 12 01
British Airways — 3 25 06 01

Lost property
Main office — 7 70 57 11
Property lost in buses and taxis — 5 23 01 11

Embassies
United Kingdom — 73 62 11
United States — 71 29 51, 71 8401
Canada — (021) 73 95 11–8

Institutions
Aliens Bureau — 3 62 83 01
Consumer Protection Centre (complaints) — 3 21 70 56
Department of Antiquities and Restoration — 3 24 30 56
Hotel Chamber — 3 23 35 01
Youth Hostel Association — 3 23 41 07, 3 23 75 90

Telegrams
Greece — 155
Abroad — 165

Telephone service
General information — 134
Directory enquiries, Athens — 131
Directory enquiries, rest of Greece — 132

Restaurants
RODIA near Lekavitos
gerofinikas KOLONAKI

Marinella
Filipos
Nikolaos